'Hail To Pitt!'

Sam Sciullo Jr.

Johnny Majors — Pitt
NATIONAL CHAMPIONS 1976 !

Tales from the

PITT PANTHERS

Sam Sciullo Jr.

www.SportsPublishingLLC.com

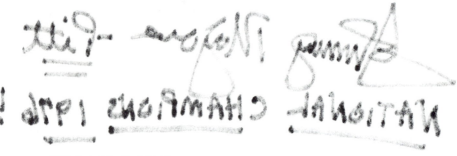

ISBN: 1-58261-198-X

Publisher: Peter L. Bannon
Senior managing editor: Susan M. Moyer
Acquisitions editor: Scott Musgrave
Developmental editor: Elisa Bock Laird
Cover/Dust jacket design: Christine Mohrbacher
Project manager: Greg Hickman
Imaging: Christine Mohrbacher
Copy editor: Cynthia L. McNew
Photo editor: Erin Linden-Levy
Vice president of sales and marketing: Kevin King
Media and promotions managers: Courtney Hainline (regional),
        Randy Fouts (national), Maurey Williamson (print)

Printed in the United States of America.

Sports Publishing L.L.C.
804 North Neil Street
Champaign, IL 61820

Phone: 1-877-424-2665
Fax: 217-363-2073
Web site: www.SportsPublishingLLC.com

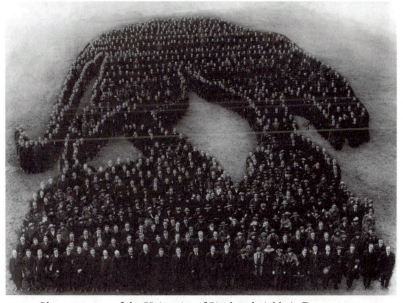

Photo courtesy of the University of Pittsburgh Athletic Department

CONTENTS

FOREWORD

If you've followed Pitt athletics for any significant length of time, you obviously have a strong heart. That's because it's been broken so many times, more so by events that took place off the field. There have been lows, but there have been many highs.

Pitt had great football teams under coaches Joe Thompson, Pop Warner, and Jock Sutherland, and later with Johnny Majors and Jackie Sherrill. It has won national championships, depending on who was doing the judging. In basketball, there were mythical national titles in two seasons. Unfortunately, most of the people who followed those teams are no longer with us. Plus, there was no *SportsCenter* back then.

The first Pitt football game I went to was in 1938, when I was seven years old. Pitt lost to Carnegie Tech at Pitt Stadium, and it was Pitt's first loss that season. That had to be one of the saddest days in school history because it knocked the Panthers out of the running for the national title, and it probably cost Marshall Goldberg the Heisman Trophy. That was his senior year, and he was part of the famous "Dream Backfield" that season. That also turned out to be Jock Sutherland's last season as Pitt's coach. I also saw the 1941 Fordham game, what I consider to be the greatest upset victory in the history of Pitt football. Jim Crowley, one of the Notre Dame Four Horsemen, was Fordham's coach.

We all waited many, many years to get basketball facilities as good as anybody's in the country. For Pitt fans, that wait became about as frustrating as it is for a mathematician to make pi come out even. Now the program is on solid ground. Let's keep it that way.

I am proud to tell people that I graduated from the University of Pittsburgh. Call it tough love. I went to work there as sports information director on July 2, 1956, a Monday. I was there through the 1965-1966 seasons. I met some great people along the way. Tom Hamilton, the athletic director who hired me, was one of them. Many of you might not know this, but he was the person who came up with one of the great sports quotes of all time: "A tie is like kissing your sister." He said it after the 1946 Army-Navy game, when a writer asked him if he had considered kicking a field goal to end the game in a tie. Tom Hamilton also did a lot for Pitt. He's the one who went out and raised the money to build the Field House and Trees Hall.

My favorite athletes during my 10 years as SID? It's not even close. Mike Ditka and Don Hennon. Ditka, he was something. He didn't just have fire in his eyes; more like a furnace. Don Hennon is a great success story. An All-American in basketball who went on to become a doctor.

Being SID at Pitt was the best job I ever had, and it was also the most fun. At the end, unfortunately, I saw what was coming. Decisions were being made by people in the administration who had absolutely no concept of what it took to play intercollegiate athletics at that level. I left just as the house was falling down. There was no doubt in my mind that I never would have lasted through the three straight 1-9 seasons. I would have either been fired or committed suicide by jumping off the top floor of the Cathedral of Learning.

Anyone who knows even a little about Pitt football knows that it had a habit of changing coaches the way some Latin American countries change dictators. The only difference was, there was no assassination on our part, although some fans probably would have wanted it. The low point for Pitt football, in my book, was the 1968 game at Notre Dame, when Ara Parseghian agreed to just let the clock run during the second half, with no stoppages.

I became even more frustrated with the university's inability to win more in basketball. That was the administration's decision. To be fair, however, Pitt wasn't the only school like that. Our friends 120 miles to the east had the same attitude about basketball for many years.

If, at any time, the university had decided to de-emphasize football and basketball, I wouldn't have been upset. Disappointed, yes, but what made me mad was they tried to go in-between. You're not always going to win. You're going to have down years. I realize that, but you have to give your kids a chance to win, and for too many years the university wasn't doing that. The foreign language requirement Pitt once had was ridiculous. To some kids—and even adults—English is a foreign language. I always felt, as Winston Churchill did, that if you knew English, you were well off.

Edward Litchfield, who was the chancellor when I worked there, did a lot of good things for Pitt, but he also lost sight of the fact that Pitt is not the school covered with Ivy League, that for a long period it was a school for many children from families of immigrants. The majority of Pitt's students came from the small towns in and around Pittsburgh and western Pennsylvania. Call it a commuter school. What's wrong with that? The Oakland community is part of what makes Pitt special, so unique.

So many colorful characters and personalities have added to Pitt's football and basketball histories. Doc Carlson. Steve Petro. Tiger Paul. Horse Czarnecki. Horse Czarnecki never finished high school, but he had more common sense than most people who have Ph.Ds.

In this book, you will read stories about glorious victories and ignominious defeats. I have known Sam Sciullo Jr. for many years, and have great respect for his knowledge and perspective of Pitt football and basketball. He has been an eyewitness to much of the good and bad that have happened. His sense of humor and irreverence remind me of me. Let that be a hint as to the theme, the mood, of this book.

—Beano Cook
April 2004

Acknowledgments

The author expresses his thanks and appreciation to the following people who shared their thoughts, memories and observations for this book:

Bernie Artman, Bill Baierl, Joe Bendel, Walt Bielich, Dean Billick, Nick Bolkovac, Jim Bolla, Charles Bonasorte, E.J. Borghetti, John Brown, Kirk Bruce, Gary Burley, Lou "Bimbo" Cecconi, Lou Cimarolli, John Cinicola, Sam Clancy, John Congemi, Carroll "Beano" Cook, Bill Daniels, Dan Daniels, Jamie Dixon, Bill Downes, Cleve Edwards, Larry Eldridge Jr., Serafino "Foge" Fazio, John Feinstein, Larry Fitzgerald, Henry Ford, Bill Fralic, Brian Generalovich, Barry Goheen, Tim Grgurich, Dick Groat, Frank Gustine Jr., Steve Halvonik, Ralph Hammond, Larry Harris, Walt Harris, Dave Hart Sr., Dave Havern, Don Hennon, Bill Hillgrove, Greg Hotchkiss, Ben Howland, Dave Janasek, Ralph Jelic, Dave Kiehl, Billy Knight, Alex Kramer, Carl Krauser, Dick Lescott, Donna (Farey) Liska, John Majors, John "Red" Manning, Mark May, Greg Meisner, Glenn Meyer, C.R. "Bob" Miller, Sean Miller, Darren Morningstar, Emil Narick, Jim O'Brien, Bill Osborn, Lou Palatella, Marino Parascenzo, Mike Paul, Whitey Rigsby, Hyman Richman, Barry Rohrssen, Dave Roman, Al Romano, Tony Salesi, Stan Savran, Sam Sciullo, Jackie Sherrill, Kimball Smith, Bob Smizik, John Swacus, Chris Taft, Bryan Thomas, Bob Timmons, Clyde Vaughan, Dick Vitale, Ron Wahl, Joe Walton, and Raymond "Bucky" Waters.

Direct quotes from individuals whose names are not listed on the previous page were derived from earlier interviews by the author.

Special thanks to E.J. Borghetti, Greg Hotchkiss, Burt Lauten, Brad Cuprik and Kristy Matus from Pitt's athletics media relations office for all their help and assistance, as well as Joe Swan from the West Virginia University sports communications office, and Sue Edson from Syracuse University. A tip of the hat to photographers Harry Bloomberg, Charles LeClaire, Will Babin (Image Point Pittsburgh) and Mike Drazdzinski, for their contributions.

CHAPTER ONE

WINNERS

Perfect Panthers

Joe Thompson played football at Pitt from 1904 to 1906, later served as a major during World War I, where he led an assault near Apremont France, and was presented with the Congressional Medal of Honor. He also became a practicing attorney in Beaver Falls, Pennsylvania.

As a football coach, Colonel Joe Thompson directed his alma mater to the only undefeated, untied, unscored upon season in school history. The 1910 Panthers went 9-0, outscoring their opponents 282-0.

The season finale that year was an 11-0 win against Penn State. *The Pittsburgh Dispatch* described the effect Thompson's pregame speech had on his players:

"The speech, which Thompson delivered to the 11 players just before they trotted on the gridiron, is said to have been a classic. If the 18,000 spectators [at Forbes Field] could have heard what he said to the men on that memorable occasion they would have voted the Beaver Falls lawyer one of the greatest exponents of the art of public speaking in the country. [They] trotted out, prepared to risk their very lives to beat [Penn] State.

Pitt's 1910 football team was undefeated, untied, and unscored upon.
Photo courtesy of the University of Pittsburgh Athletic Department

"Thompson's hand was seen at every stage of the game. At the start it was his orders that the scrub-eleven trotted out on the field. ... It has long been State's plan to allow the local team to go out on the field when they often chilled before the first whistle blew. When the scrubs trotted out yesterday, it completely fooled the Up-Staters, who after waiting followed them, only to find that the Pitt regulars had not yet made their appearance."

The Great Orator Gets His Comeuppance

The football teams at Pitt and Georgia Tech were in 1918 what LSU and Southern California might have been in 2004—a game the public demanded.

Football fans throughout the South were awed by coach John Heisman's Georgia Tech teams from that era. They won games by outrageous scores, including a 222-0 victory against Cumberland in 1917.

In Pittsburgh, meanwhile, Pop Warner had taken over at Pitt in 1915, and his first three seasons were a perfect 26-0. The Panthers opened the 1918 campaign with wins against Washington & Jefferson (34-0) and Penn (37-0), setting up a clash with Heisman's Georgia Tech team at a jam-packed Forbes Field on October 23.

Heisman, a public speaker of note who also dabbled as a Shakespearean actor in his spare time, had his teams utilize a series of shifting movements.

"You must learn to hop like a chickadee," Heisman was quoted as saying in Robert Leckie's *The Story of Football.*

Warner hated the finesse game, calling Heisman's brand of football "fancy movement such as is necessary for the success of a Russian toe dancer."

According to Leckie's account, the teams dressed in adjacent locker rooms, separated only by a thin wall. While Heisman made an impassioned plea to his players, the Panthers prepared themselves quietly. Legend has it that Warner motioned for his players to come to the wall to listen to Heisman's speech.

"Okay, boys, you heard that," Warner said. "Go out and tear 'em up."

Pitt won 32-0 and defeated Tech 16-6 in a rematch the next year.

A Pair of All-Americans on One Quintet

Pitt had not one, but two, All-Americans as members of its 21-0 national championship basketball team of 1927-1928. Both Charley Hyatt and Sykes Reed earned All-America honors from Helms Foundation, and, many years later, Reed spoke with pride about the type of basketball played during his time.

"We broke faster and came down court quicker than they do now," Reed said in a 1950 interview with *The Pittsburgh Press.* "Most of the time, it took us one pass to get to mid-court, and then a couple of more for a shot. This wouldn't always work, but we could stop and then work the ball in under the hoop."

Pop Warner coached Panthers football from 1915 to 1923.
Photo courtesy of the University of Pittsburgh Athletic Department

Reed, who stood six feet tall, had high praise for the illustrious Hyatt, who was the same size.

"Charley Hyatt would score 50 points a game today," Reed boasted. "And you don't need much more than that to win."

Playing for Jock Sutherland

For many young football players growing up in the Pennsylvania-Ohio-West Virginia tri-state area during the 1930s, Pitt was it.

"We were so excited about Pitt at the time," said Emil Narick, who came to Pitt in 1936, a national championship season. "I think most kids, and especially those who were football players in high school, were hoping and praying to receive a football scholarship to the University of Pittsburgh. We knew all about Jock Sutherland, the famous football coach, and his great teams that played games all over the country."

Narick, who was from Benwood, West Virginia, a mining town adjacent to Wheeling, had his enthusiasm for Pitt boosted in the classroom as well.

"There was a great football player at Pitt in the '30s named Charles Hartwig," Narick recalled, "and he had a sister who was one of our teachers in high school. She would talk about him, and his Pitt experience, quite a bit, and we found all that to be very interesting."

Narick's scholarship wish was granted, and he made his way to Pittsburgh to meet the legendary coach and his new teammates.

"I took a bus to Pittsburgh for the start of training camp," he said. "It was a Saturday morning when I arrived. I remember the first person I saw was [Marshall] Biggie Goldberg. He recognized me because he had played basketball against me in high school. Marshall was from Elkins, West Virginia. He said to me, 'Hiya Snake, how ya doin'?' Snake used to be the nickname for the teams at West Virginia [University]."

Narick was about to discover what Goldberg, who was entering his sophomore season at Pitt, and the rest of the Panthers already knew about their coach.

"He was the kind of person who, in his own way, imparted to the players that they were to conduct themselves a certain way," said Narick. "He didn't have to tell me or any of my teammates what to do or what not to do."

Goldberg had a similar recollection.

"I was in awe the first time I met him," he said. "He was a very impressive man. He was very dour, very soldierly, upright, prim and serious. I had to get real close to him to understand what he was saying. He spoke with a strong Scottish accent. The more I was around him, the more I liked him."

"He was real stoic," said Bob Timmons, who played for Sutherland during the 1930s. "He was a bachelor, and he didn't say too much. You liked him, though. He didn't whack you or cuss you out. He didn't treat you like a slave. If you screwed up, he would demote you, but he didn't demean you. He was a gentleman."

For Narick, there wasn't any need to position himself close to Sutherland. He admits he never had a genuine conversation with the coach during their three years together.

"We had one very serious conversation that I like to tell people about," Narick said. "[Sutherland's] last year, spring training of 1938, we were running the single wing at practice. I was the right halfback and Dick Cassiano was left halfback. Ben Kish was quarterback. On this particular play I was supposed to block the end, which I did so well that I knocked myself out cold, for about 30 seconds. When I came to, I walked back, groggily, to the huddle, when Doctor Sutherland came over to me and said, 'Good block, Narick.'"

Sutherland's players treated their coach with the utmost respect, and he reciprocated that feeling in kind.

"He treated me like a son," Goldberg said. "He wanted to know how I felt. He didn't want me to practice on Fridays, the day before a game. I never asked him for anything. When I came out before my senior year [1938] and told him that I would switch from halfback to fullback so Dick Cassiano could be better utilized, he was overwhelmed."

*Jock Sutherland (center) won more games (111) than
any coach in Pitt history. At far left is assistant coach Bill Kern.*
Photo courtesy of the University of Pittsburgh Athletic Department

The Panthers of that era understood their place as representatives of the University of Pittsburgh.

"We always said, 'Yes, Doctor' or 'No, Doctor,'" Narick said. "We knew that he expected our best at all times. You knew that you had to go to class. You knew that you had to keep your grades up, and you knew that you had to be conditioned. You also had to be totally disciplined. He never tolerated anybody talking back to officials. You accepted what they said. He also didn't want anybody jumping around or celebrating. When you scored a touchdown, you handed the ball back to the official."

Life on campus for Pitt players then was less regimented than it eventually became for college football players.

"There were no athletic dorms or any type of dorms," Narick said. "I lived in a rooming house at first, before I joined a fraternity and lived there. The players were on their own the night before a home game. We policed ourselves. Back then, all the games started around one or one-thirty. The one routine we had was the day of the game, when we always met at the Schenley Hotel [now the William Pitt Union] for our pregame meal. It was a big meal–steaks, eggs, you name it. It was usually pretty quiet during that time, mainly because we were eating! I could never dream of ever having that type of meal before that."

For road trips, the Panthers normally went by train, and Narick remembers that Sutherland would customarily have a couple of his friends from the Pittsburgh Athletic Association (PAA) accompany the team on the trip.

"We were expected to dress neatly, usually a jacket and tie," Narick said. "We would always go for a walk well before the game, and Doctor Sutherland would lead us in that. And when it was time to play the game, we knew exactly what we were expected to do, because he had prepared us so well."

Narick recognized that Sutherland was a master at organization.

"The assistant coaches were really the ones we had genuine conversations with," he said. "They did most of the actual instructing. Doctor Sutherland was the overseer of everything."

Everyone Called Him "Mike"

Pitt's football teams compiled back-to-back 6-3 seasons in 1948 and 1949, but their efforts and accomplishments aren't as popular to recall when fans and writers reminisce. Much of the success for those teams can be attributed to their coach, Mike Milligan, whose first name was actually Walter.

"[Milligan] is, in my lifetime, the least appreciated Pitt football coach," Alex Kramer said.

Milligan had played for Pitt under Jock Sutherland and was top assistant to Panthers' coach Wes Fesler in 1946. He took over at Pitt the following year, where he remained through the 1949 season. During his summers in college, Milligan worked as a desk sergeant with the Aliquippa (Pennsylvania) Police Department.

"If you're looking for Knute Rockne or Woody Hayes-type stories about Mike, you're probably not going to find them," said Nick Bolkovac, who played for Milligan's Panthers. "That's probably why he didn't have the reputation that some others [coaches] may have had."

Bolkovac remembered Milligan as the type of person whose antics could come across as being comical, though not intentionally.

"He was very down to earth and real," Bolkovac said. "I had an awful lot of respect for the guy.

"He would get down and try to demonstrate how to pull and do things, and he would go through the motions in three-quarters time. We found that rather humorous, yet he was effective in what he was trying to coach."

Milligan's finest hour as Pitt football coach may have been late in the 1948 season. The Panthers, who had upset Ohio State—coached by Fesler—in Pittsburgh the year before, were whipped in all facets of the game, 41-0, in the 1948 rematch. The Panthers, bruised and battered, had a road date with Purdue the next week before hosting Penn State in the season finale at Pitt Stadium.

Pitt defeated the Boilermakers 20-13, setting up a showdown with the undefeated Nittany Lions, who were riding a 17-game unbeaten streak.

"We were grossly undermanned that day," said Bolkovac, whose interception return for a touchdown in the fourth quarter was the only score in Pitt's 7-0 upset win. "Mike did something in that game that went a long way toward our victory. Bill Hardisty had a great game punting us out of trouble. When Penn State had the ball deep in its territory, Mike would pull some of us frontliners out—give us a few minutes break—until Penn State got the ball back on our end of the field. Then he'd put us back in again, and it worked. We were able to stop them. That's a little nuance that most people weren't aware of."

Milligan resigned following a 6-3 season in 1949. He never coached after that.

"[The Pitt administration] offered him a one-year contract, and Mike thought he deserved better," Bolkovac said. "That's why he left."

"To Mike, football ceased being played in 1949," Kramer said. "I can't recall any bitterness that he felt toward Pitt, but he was not a fan of football after that. He did not have a high opinion of how it was being played."

Signs of the Times

Not all members of Pitt's football team were welcomed with open arms when the Panthers traveled to Houston and Miami in 1951 to play games against Rice and Miami, respectively.

"Special arrangements had to be made ahead of time for the few blacks who were on the team to stay in the homes of black professionals in those cities," recalled Alex Kramer, the team's manager. "The Shamrock Hotel in Houston would not accept black people. But, as I recall, there was no protest [by the Pitt people]. It was something that was just accepted. Nobody spoke out about it."

Bobby Epps and Henry Ford were Pitt's lone black players that season. Ford recalled the experience.

"We were separated from the rest of the team several times that year," he said. "Back then, it was accepted, and we learned how to deal with it. There was nothing we could do about it."

Ford, who had the same experience on the road in professional football, remembered how and when the black Pitt players discovered that they wouldn't be with the rest of their teammates in the South.

"We weren't told about it until we were on the planes on the way down there," he said. "The coach, Red Dawson, would tell us."

Four seasons later, a much greater public furor arose when Pitt's Bobby Grier became the first black to play at the annual Sugar Bowl game in New Orleans. Grier stayed in a motel that catered to blacks. He, however, gained a certain level of celebrity over the entire episode and speaks fondly of the experience in general.

"I did have a good time at the Sugar Bowl," he said, years later in an interview with *Inside Panthers Sports Magazine.* "I belonged to a national black fraternity, Kappa Alpha Psi, and the fraternity invited me to parties at a couple black colleges down there. They were Xavier and Dillard. They couldn't have been any nicer to me. I had a great time."

Pitt fans questioned how nice the officials were to Grier and the Panthers during the game. Georgia Tech won 7-0, and the only touchdown of the game resulted from a pass interference penalty called against Grier in the first quarter of play.

"It Was Like a Palace Compared to What We Played in Before"

There was no great debate about constructing a new sports facility on campus. No voter referendum was required to settle any argument about the continued viability of the old Pitt Stadium Pavilion.

"We used to call The Pavilion 'The Icebox,'" said Bernie Artman, a Pitt basketball player during that era. "We had to warm up with our warmups on all the way until the game started, that's how cold it was in there. It was a terrible place to play. There was a dirt floor leading from the dressing room to the court, so you always had to wipe your feet before you started to play."

Artman was drawn to Pitt by his older brother, Bob, who had played for coach Doc Carlson and the Panthers—and by the lure of the new building.

"I had offers from a number of schools," Bernie Artman said, "but my brother told me, 'Go to Pitt, because they're building this new field house.' When we went up there and saw it, it was like a palace compared to what we played in before."

The mood was festive when Pitt christened what was then known as Memorial Field House on December 15, 1951. Columbia, which had been 22-1 the year before, was the Panthers' first opponent. Carlson, dribbling a basketball, led the Panthers across the court under a spotlight's glare before the opening tip. Artman was the star of the show, hitting a late basket to give the Panthers a 65-64 victory.

"There was a lot of excitement in that first game," he said. "I just happened to get lucky and score the last bucket."

"Let's Win One for the Panthers!"

What better place than Notre Dame Stadium for an underdog football team to receive an inspirational pep talk. The Pitt Panthers were a two-touchdown underdog heading into their game at Notre Dame on October 11, 1952.

"The thing that stuck in my mind was what our coach, Red Dawson said," Dick Deitrick recalls. "He said two things to us: 'You know, they're no different from you guys. You both put your pants on one leg at a time.' And he said, 'Father Leahy—he called [Notre Dame coach] Frank Leahy, Father Leahy—he has this defense that he thinks is the greatest, and it's not worth a damn.'"

But it was Pitt's quiet leader, linebacker Joe Schmidt, who—uncharacteristically—stole the show. He asked Dawson to please leave the room. He had a few things he wanted to say.

"He said, 'Hey, these Notre Dame guys think you're nothing,'" teammate Merle DeLuca remembered. "'They're laughing at us.' Joe also said a few things I'm not going to repeat."

"I'm not too much on making speeches," said Schmidt, nearly a half-century later. "But for some reason, it just seemed the right time to say something. I don't think totally that we believed in ourselves, that we were good enough to beat Notre Dame. My thinking was that someone just needed to make some common sense remarks about the fact that most of us were from western Pennsylvania, and that a lot of us had been All-State in high school, that we're good football players. Notre Dame had quite a few players from our area, and most of our guys had played against them in high school and were just as good as they were. It was just an awakening to the fact that, 'Hey, we're damned good football players, and we can do the job.'"

The Panthers won the game 22-19, with Notre Dame missing a field goal that would have tied it late in the fourth quarter.

Michelosen Didn't Say Much

John Michelosen had played football at Pitt for coach Jock Sutherland and later served as his assistant with the Pittsburgh Steelers. When Sutherland died in 1948, Michelosen replaced him as head coach of the Steelers. It seems the two shared some personality traits.

"[Michelosen] hardly talked to anybody," said Ralph Jelic, who played for Michelosen during the coach's first two seasons [1955 and 1956] as Pitt's head man. "He would walk back and forth, back and forth, during practices and games, rarely saying anything. He might come over and quietly say something to a kid. The players thought he was unapproachable."

Unapproachable, maybe; respected, yes.

"John Michelosen was a man of few words, but he was a very sound football coach," said Bimbo Cecconi, who was an assistant under him. "Could you block and tackle? Do it over and over again. Repetition. He had that single-wing mentality when it came to football."

"I liked [Michelosen]," Lou Cimarolli said. "Mike was always laid back. He was used to coaching in the pros, where it's a different type of player. He had us well taught. The motivation part was up to you."

Michelosen's low-key style was in stark contrast to the type of coaching Cimarolli was accustomed to while playing at Bridgeville (Pennsylvania) High School.

"The coach I had in high school was all fire and what-not," he said. "Then I got to Pitt and had John Michelosen, but [John] and I got along real well."

"John Michelosen was an excellent football coach," said Joe Walton, who was on the team when Michelosen took over. "We were very well-versed in the fundamentals. What I learned from him held me in good stead throughout my career."

Jelic's Rule-Changing Punt

Some clever maneuvering by Pitt punter Ralph Jelic in the 1955 season opener led to a rule change in college football.

Both Jelic and Pitt coach John Michelosen were making their debuts on September 17, 1955, when the Panthers hosted the California Golden Bears at Pitt Stadium.

"In those days teams didn't have any specialists the way they do today," Jelic said. "As far as punting and extra points and things like that, you just took whoever could do it. We had a guy, Bill Schmitt, whose nickname was 'Big Boy,' who could really punt. It was amazing how high and how far he could punt a football."

But, in the 1950s, that wasn't always the best thing.

"Back then, if the punt would go in the end zone, the team kicking the ball would lose yardage," Jelic said. "In that game, we were on about our own 40, and Schmitt said, 'Why not let Jelic kick this one?'"

The results were Football Follies material.

"The center snapped the ball over my head, and I had to run all the way back to about the five to pick it up," Jelic said. "I started to run with it with two or three Cal guys chasing me. Their player hits me as I'm kicking it. It ends up being a 57-yard punt."

Cal was called for roughing the kicker, and Pitt maintained possession with a first down.

"Their coach was a guy named Pappy Waldorf, who was a real character," Jelic said. "He was arguing about the call. Instead of them getting the ball at our five—we were down 7-0 at the time—we kept the ball. Because of that play, the rule regarding a punter taking off with the ball was changed. He became fair game."

Pitt defeated the Golden Bears 27-7.

The Great Jim Brown
Met Strong Pitt Resistance

On nights before home games, coach John Michelosen would take his players to the movies.

"We would go to a private studio on the Boulevard of the Allies to watch films," Ralph Jelic said. "It was a way to keep us isolated. You never saw any films back then, so it was a big deal to see these Hollywood pictures. The night before we played Syracuse here [1956], we were watching films of Jimmy Brown against Colgate. He was just dominating. That stirred us up. We wanted to get at him."

The Panthers had limited the Orangemen—and Brown—to 98 yards rushing in a 22-12 win at Syracuse the year before. This would be Brown's last crack at the Panthers.

Pitt won again 14-7 at Pitt Stadium. Brown carried the ball 14 times for 52 yards.

"He never did anything against us," Jelic said.

Lou Cimarolli played in the 1955 game and remembers one play in particular.

"We were in a 5-4 defense, and John Paluck was the end lined up in front of me," Cimarolli said. "One time Brown took the ball and John hit him and grabbed hold right in his midsection. I had an opportunity to come up and finish him off, so I took a shot and hit him right across the head. [Brown] was a big horse; I remember that."

"[Brown] was a great player, but we had some pretty good teams, and we held our own against him," Joe Walton added.

Brown did gain some measure of revenge against the Panthers in a different sport, but that's a story for another chapter.

Hennon's First Game—34 at NC State

Don Hennon had the kind of collegiate basketball debut players dream about: 34 points in a 97-85 loss at North Carolina State on December 1, 1956. Did Hennon, then a sophomore, sneak up on the unsuspecting Wolfpack?

"Your first game, the other team doesn't really know about you, but NC State should have known about me," Hennon said. "I had visited there with [coach] Everett Case. They had a whole notebook on me. Those [Atlantic Coast Conference] schools were way ahead of the competition in recruiting at that time. They had statistics and press clippings from practically all your games in high school."

Still, Hennon surprised the opposition—but not Pitt's other opponents that season.

"The players didn't seem to guard me as closely in that first game as they did the next game," Hennon said. "But that NC State game was fun. It was a great experience, and a nice way to start a career."

The General Versus Senator Bradley

Smarting from an 86-85 loss at Miami in the finals of the Hurricane Classic three days earlier, Brian Generalovich and the Panthers returned to Pittsburgh to face Bill Bradley and the Princeton Tigers at the Pitt Field House on December 31, 1962.

"It was one of the most physical, brutal one-on-ones I ever witnessed," Pitt guard Dave Roman said. "It was like a football game between those two. They banged the whole time. They spent part of the game on the floor."

Generalovich was known as a bruiser; Bradley's game leaned toward finesse.

"He wasn't a very physical player," Generalovich said. "When he would come inside, we would get physical with him. Bill was very smooth."

The Panthers won the game 71-62.

"They were never really in the game," said Generalovich, who then struck up a friendship with Bradley. At the end of that season, both Pitt and Princeton found themselves at the Penn Palestra in Philadelphia for the opening round of the NCAA tourmament.

"I sat with Bill the night before our game, watching other games," Generalovich said. "He was a real gentleman. I never kept up with him after that, but you could tell he was destined to do something, maybe politically."

Weird Weather and the Lucky Stone

Pitt traveled to Los Angeles to open the 1963 football season against UCLA, and assistant coach Bimbo Cecconi decided to take a walk on the beach the day before the game.

"I saw a stone on the beach, and I decided to take it," Cecconi said. "I showed it to [quarterback] Fred [Mazurek] and said, 'Freddie, I'm gonna keep this stone because this is gonna be our lucky stone throughout the year.'"

Cecconi might have been better off if he had kept his find a secret—from Mazurek, at least.

"Freddie was a worry-wart," Cecconi said. "He was very superstitious. He took everything to heart."

All was well with Pitt and its lucky charm—until the Panthers played at Navy in the fifth week.

"After warmups before that game, we were back in the locker room, and Mazurek asked me, 'Coach, do you have the stone?' And I didn't have the stone. But I said, 'Don't worry about it, Fred. We'll be okay.'"

The Panthers were not okay. They were stuck in neutral for much of the game, and lost 24-12.

"That was his worst game of the year," Cecconi recalled. "I remember we had to use [backup quarterback] Kenny Lucas a little bit to try a few things. But the fact that I didn't have the stone with me bothered Fred. That affected him."

Cecconi kept the stone in a drawer at his home and brought it to the rest of Pitt's games—all victories—the rest of the season.

"The stone was part of our lore that year," he said.

It received its greatest test on November 2 when Syracuse came to Pitt Stadium.

"We went out and worked out before the game," Cecconi said, "and when we went back out, there was an inch of snow on the ground. Here comes Fred. 'Coach, look at the snow on the ground. What are we gonna do?' I said, 'Freddie, they don't call off football games. We're playing this game.' He was a nervous wreck."

Playing in weather that alternated from sun to snow to thunder and lightning, back to sunshine, the Panthers came from behind to defeat Syracuse 35-27. Mazurek ran for 119 yards and passed for 136.

"It was the oddest game, weather-wise, I ever saw," Cecconi said. "And Fred played one helluva game because he didn't want to get hit. He didn't want to be down on the ground."

Bob Smizik wrote for *The Pitt News* that year, and he remembers that day well.

"That morning [*The Pitt News*] played the Syracuse student newspaper in a game of touch football at Schenley Oval," Smizik said. "We played in T-shirts. A few of us showered and changed at *The Pitt News* offices. As we left for the game, it had cooled considerably. By game time it was downright chilly, and eventually it started to snow. What had been a glorious morning turned into a downright awful day."

Many years later, at a reunion to honor Pitt's "No-Bowl" team, Cecconi presented the stone to Mazurek. He retains a soft spot for the ever-serious Mazurek, whose personality complemented the rest of that unique team.

"Paul Martha, Rick Leeson, and those guys were wild," Cecconi said. "They were outgoing city kids, and they knew how to live it up and enjoy life. They liked to tease Fred about his romance with Sue Michelosen [daughter of the head coach, John Michelosen]. But Fred was a great kid. He was the kind of guy you wanted on your team."

Ridl's Runnin' Panthers

Buzz Ridl had written a book titled *How To Develop A Deliberate Offense,* but it's doubtful his Panthers referred to its principles prior to Pitt's February 13, 1970, game against Syracuse at Fitzgerald Field House. The Panthers registered a school single-game scoring record in defeating the Orangemen 127-108.

"It certainly was out of character for the way that we normally played," Mike Paul remembered. "[Syracuse] kind of forced it because of the way they played defense. They sold out on our end of the court by committing three guys."

Paul and his Panther teammates were surprised that Syracuse stuck to its plan without making any type of adjustments.

"They pressed us the whole time," he said. "I brought the ball in by throwing it to Billy [Downes]. They came up to trap us, we threw it over the top and it was a two-on-one break the whole way, the whole game."

Cleve Edwards, Pitt's point guard that night, tells a slightly different story.

"We weren't as big as Syracuse, so we couldn't set up and pound it inside against them," Edwards said. "We ran something called 'The Albany Shuffle.' I told Mike Patcher a few days before that game, 'You [rebound] the ball, get it to me, and I'll get you 20 points against these guys. We started running, and we never stopped."

The Panthers led at halftime 58-37.

"In the locker room, Coach Ridl finished talking," Edwards said. "On the way out, he stopped me. He said, 'Listen, you proved your point. Now we're gonna go back and do it the way we talked about doing it.' I said, 'Coach, I don't know how to do nothing else but run. If you don't want me to run, don't put me in.'"

The Panthers went out and scored 69 points in the second half. Syracuse scored 71!

Despite the record-setting numbers, the quick-scoring method limited at least one Panther's average that night.

"I couldn't get across half court before our team put it up," Paul said. "I couldn't get any shots. I thought to myself, 'Syracuse isn't playing any defense, and I can't even get into the offense!'"

Kent Scott led the Panthers with 28 points, followed by Paul O'Gorek (27) and Edwards (20 points, 13 assists). The memorable game—played on a Friday night—was witnessed by only 1,192 spectators, but a group of Pitt students showed its appreciation afterward.

"When we got back to our dorm room, at Tower A, both nets had been cut down and were hanging on our door," said Paul, who roomed with Downes. "We lived on a floor with a bunch of engineering majors, and they decided to do that for us."

Forget the Farewell Party

West Virginia University athletics officials had planned a grand sendoff to their old basketball field house—including the playing of "Auld Lang Syne"—following an expected win against Pitt on March 3, 1970. Buzz Ridl's Panthers, however, crashed the party.

The game went according to WVU's script at the outset, with the Mountaineers jumping to a 19-point lead in the first half. But Pitt, trying to win its third straight game to finish the season at .500 (12-12), made a furious rally in the second half.

"Kent Scott just lit it up after halftime," said Mike Paul, a sophomore that season. "He couldn't miss."

Scott scored 32 points overall, including 23 after intermission to give Pitt its first win in Morgantown since 1963. It also represented the Panthers' first non-losing season since 1963-1964 and made one Panther in particular very grateful.

"After the game, [now deceased] Mike Patcher—what a great guy—came up to Kent Scott and me as we were getting dressed and said, 'I just want to tell you guys thanks.' I said, 'For what?' He said, 'Because this game tonight made sticking it out for four years worth it.' Mike was one of the few guys from the Bob Timmons era who stuck it out and played for Buzz."

And what about the postgame celebration?

"They cancelled it," Billy Downes remembered. "They didn't even play the song."

"Everybody just got up and left," said Bill Hillgrove, then completing his first season as Pitt's radio play-by-play man. "They were absolutely stunned."

Paving the Way for Young Dorsett

Dave Janasek was one of the holdovers from the Carl DePasqua years, a veteran fullback who was looking forward to a fresh start with a new coach, Johnny Majors. Majors was coming to a program that had posted a 1-10 record in 1972.

"It's not that we didn't have some decent athletes with DePasqua," Janasek said, "but [the early 1970s] was an interesting time. The discipline under DePasqua was there, but it was pretty wild in Oakland then. When Johnny got there, he put the clamps on us and forced us to focus on football."

Included in Majors's massive first recruiting class was a freshman tailback named Tony Dorsett.

"When Tony got there, that gave us the explosive back that we needed," Janasek said. "We had some decent runners, but nobody like Tony Dorsett."

Janasek and his older teammates had an early preview of how different Pitt football would be. Before leaving for training camp at Johnstown, the coaching staff put the players through some light workouts on the home campus.

"The coaches lined us up to get our times in the 40," he said. "They had all the returning players in one line, and all the freshmen and junior college players in another. One of the coaches would announce your name for you to go up and do your sprint.

Everybody was going along until the coach said, 'Tony Dorsett.' Everybody just stopped to watch. He did it in four-four, or something like that."

Dorsett further impressed his new team by executing a long run in the team's first scrimmage at camp.

"I remember Johnny Majors jumping up and down on the sideline, yelling something like, 'We have a tailback! We have a tailback!'" Janasek recalled.

Janasek had done a little running for Pitt in 1972, but one look at Dorsett told him the Panthers' offense was going to be centered around one player. He wasn't disappointed.

"I realized I had a pretty good knack for blocking, particularly the roll block going around the ends," Janasek said. "And going up the middle. I liked hitting, taking on inside linebackers, and Tony was so good at reading blocks, he would cut right off."

The veteran Panthers came to realize that, in many ways, Dorsett was their meal ticket in 1973. As such, he deserved the special considerations accorded.

"He was so light that first year; he was banged up all the time," Janasek said. "A lot of weeks he wouldn't practice until Thursdays. Some people might get a little upset with that, but with him it was, 'Hey, get healthy, practice when you can, and let's get ready to win on Saturday.'"

"I was getting tattooed," said Dorsett describing the punishment he took as a runner that first season. It reached a point where the freshman sensation seriously considered quitting. Myrtle Dorsett—Tony's mother—and assistant coach Jackie Sherrill were the ones who were able to talk him out of it.

"Jackie Sherrill would say to me, 'Hawk, we need you,'" Dorsett recalled.

Dorsett and Janasek, the starting backs in Pitt's offenses in 1973 and 1974, developed a good relationship. They were roommates the nights before games during those two seasons and shared a dorm room at Pitt-Johnstown at 1974's training camp.

"We talked about things," Janasek said. "We were actually dating girls who lived next to each other in one dorm. We were decent friends then, and we're friends now."

"It Was a Pride Thing"

More than 100 players arrived at Pitt's Johnstown campus in August 1973 for new coach Johnny Majors's first training camp. Approximately half of the campers hadn't been in the program the previous season, including junior college transfer Gary Burley, a defensive lineman who had played at Wharton Junior College in Texas.

"It was like a family being brought together," Burley said. "It was a melting pot of football players from around the country who finally got to a place they could call their own and to develop something. I don't think we knew at the time that we were on the verge of restarting Pitt football."

But there was a steep price to pay. Majors and his energetic assistants put the team through a demanding camp.

"Johnstown was a tough camp," Burley said. "That was as tough a camp as I've ever been around."

Too tough for some of the troops.

"I remember players jumping off the roof of the dorm overnight so they didn't have to be seen leaving—quitting—the next morning," Burley said. "It was a pride thing. Guys didn't want to quit in front of the other players, so they would sneak out in the middle of the night."

Majors, who was noted for his catchy phrases, liked to say, "Those who stay will play, and those who stay will be champions."

Burley recalled another Majors saying, one that summarized what the first-year coach and his staff were trying to impart to the players that summer.

"'Stick to your knitting,' he liked to tell us," Burley said. "'Do the little things, and the big things will take care of themselves.'"

Southern Hospitality

Vince Dooley was concerned. He had a hunch his Georgia Bulldogs were in for a fight when they opened the 1973 season at home against the new-look Pitt Panthers.

"We were in a very dangerous and precarious position going into that game," Dooley said many years later.

Pitt had a horde of new players ready to be unleashed, most notably Tony Dorsett.

"We knew going in what type of player Dorsett was in high school," Dooley said, "but the guy who made an even greater impact that day was the nose guard [Gary Burley] they had recruited from a junior college in Texas. He gave us all kinds of trouble. He caused all kinds of havoc."

Rusty Russell, who later became an assistant coach at Pitt during John Majors's second term, was a Bulldog defensive back in that opening game on September 15, 1973. He also remembers Burley's contributions to the 7-7 tie.

"We couldn't handle Burley at all," Russell said. "He was in our backfield all day."

Burley remembers the camaraderie the Pitt players and staff felt before that game.

"We pulled into the stadium, and there's a place there [Sanford Stadium] that they call The Cliff," Burley said. "The buses from the opposing team park there. It's adjacent to the stadium. Up above, there's an overlook where people can look down. I saw all these fans with red shirts and Confederate flags. We didn't know what we were getting into."

Just before the team's walkthrough, Burley called an impromptu session with his teammates.

"I pulled all the guys together and we said a prayer," he said. "I remember saying, 'Hey, we're just about the only people here who are going to support us.' In the locker room right before the game, we really weren't sure what to expect. We were like a bunch of nomads who had come together under Coach Majors and the crew."

Pitt stunned the Bulldog crowd, taking a 7-0 lead on a touchdown run by quarterback Billy Daniels. Dorsett, in his collegiate debut, ran for 100 yards. Eventually, the Georgia crowd lost its hard edge.

"The crowd was silent later in the game," Burley recalled. "I'll always remember how silent that stadium became."

The Panthers were somewhat content with the 7-7 tie in unfriendly territory.

"I think that's where that Pitt team came together," Burley said.

The Calmest Man in Columbia

Having had their 22-game winning streak snapped in a heart-breaking last-second loss at Penn State four days earlier, the 1973-1974 Panthers didn't have much time to feel sorry for themselves when they played at one of college basketball's toughest venues, the University of South Carolina. Pitt lost to the Gamecocks 67-50 but learned a valuable lesson about poise and self-control.

"That was a hostile place to play, a really tough environment," Kirk Bruce said. "The crowd was extremely loud, and our bench was right in front of their student section. The thing I remember was the way coach [Buzz] Ridl handled himself and the team. During time-outs, he would be kneeling with his back to the crowd, while we were facing the students. They were throwing all kinds of things at us—paper balls, jawbreakers, everything. Some of us were ready to go after somebody. Coach Ridl was getting pelted with this stuff, too, but he never flinched, never turned around to see what it was or who it was. He just kept his focus, very calmly telling us what we had to do as far as the game."

Missing Players in Annapolis

College football coaches can be a bit edgy at times, particularly the night before a big game, so when Al Romano and several other players were nowhere to be found the day before Pitt's 1976 game at Navy, there was genuine alarm.

"The coaches were uptight all week going into that game," said Romano, the team's starting nose tackle. "We had lost to them the year before at home, plus [quarterback] Matt [Cavanaugh] was still out with an injury."

Following the team's arrival in Annapolis on Friday afternoon, one of the players, who had some relatives in the area, coaxed several players, including Romano, to go with him to visit his family.

"We all got back late for the team meal the night before the game, and let's just say the coaches weren't too happy with us," Romano said. "They were on pins and needles as it was. I don't want to condone what we did. We were late, and we deserved whatever punishment we received, but my point is we had so much confidence in ourselves and knew how good we were that we just went out and beat Navy [45-0] without any trouble."

"Hurley Ran Us Ragged"

Two plays that produced zero yards were most vital in Pitt's march to the 1976 college football national championship.

Coming off a 45-0 win at Navy, a game in which Tony Dorsett became the NCAA's all-time rushing yardage leader, the Panthers may have been too relaxed and confident getting ready for Syracuse at Pitt Stadium the following Saturday. One Panther, however, was wary.

Al Romano, who was from the Syracuse area (Solvay, New York), tried to warn his teammates about the approaching danger, especially Syracuse sophomore quarterback Bill Hurley.

"I told people that Hurley could hurt us, that he could run all over the place," Romano said.

The Panthers were in their most precarious position that season, nursing a 20-13 lead midway through the fourth quarter. The Orangemen had the ball at the Pitt 11. It was third down, one yard to go.

"[Syracuse] ran what we call a two-hole," Romano said. "When Hurley ran that, I took out the guard, but the center shot out for [linebacker] Arnie Weatherington. Arnie was to the right side of the

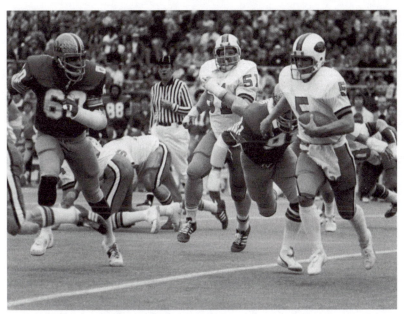

Cecil Johnson (left) and Al Romano (in close pursuit) had their hands full chasing Syracuse quarterback Bill Hurley (5) when Pitt defeated the Orangemen in the 1976 game at Pitt Stadium.
Photo courtesy of the University of Pittsburgh Athletic Department

center, to the wide side of the field. The center tried to get a piece of me, but I slowed him up. I remember being at the bottom of the pile and grabbing for ankles. I figured, 'This guy [fullback Jim Sessler] ain't going another foot.' But it was Arnie who made the great play. He stood the guy up."

The spot had the ball just short of a first down. It was there, Romano offers, that Syracuse might have had a beef.

"If he did make the first down, it was on the third-down play," he said.

That set up the crucial fourth-and-one attempt.

"I was on one knee, and I was exhausted," Romano said. "That SOB Hurley had run me and everyone else on that defense out of gas."

To bolster the interior line, offensive lineman Joe Stone entered the game, a move that shifted Romano over a notch.

"That put me in the two-gap," he said. "Hurley called that audible, 'Red, 32! Red, 32!' It was the same play! So I yelled to Arnie, who was again lined up to right, 'Arnie: Two! Two!' On the film, you'll see my arm pointing in that direction."

Sure enough, Sessler took the handoff from Hurley.

"I shot the gap, and I could see the bottom of the football as he was getting it," Romano said. "I went for his legs. In a millisecond, [three] things went through my head: first down; touchdown; game tied. If I could have taken both his legs off with my hands, I would have done it right then and there."

The Panthers had survived their toughest test that season, then drove downfield for a Carson Long game-clinching field goal. Pitt won 23-13. Romano—and Hurley—still think about that dramatic sequence. They usually see each other at least once a year, often at a golf outing hosted by Tony Dorsett.

"Hurley still nods his head, as if to say, 'Yes,' and I shake my head, 'No,'" Romano said. "It's an ongoing thing, this many years later."

No Easy Time for Majors

Going down the stretch of the 1976 football season was a thrilling—albeit confusing—time for coach John Majors, who was being recruited by his alma mater, Tennessee, to return as its new football coach.

"I wanted to stay a lot more than I wanted to go but, you know, to try to revive your alma mater, I had family there, but I was very happy here in Pittsburgh," Majors said. "I didn't want to go anywhere. I can't say that I've regretted it—I really can't—because I had some great, exciting times at Tennessee and some great days."

Majors admitted that the tug of Pittsburgh remained strong, well after he'd returned to Knoxville.

"The first two or three years after I left here, when I'd come back through that [Fort Pitt] tunnel for recruiting or to visit friends, my heart hurt, because I knew what we'd left here, and I knew what we had to try to get done at Tennessee. It really hurt for two or three years, and I didn't get it out of my system as quickly as I should have."

To compound the curious circumstances, Majors accepted the Tennessee job one week after Pitt wrapped up the regular season at 11-0 and a No. 1 ranking by beating Penn State at Three Rivers Stadium. He spent a couple weeks in December commuting back and forth between Pittsburgh and Knoxville, before leaving for New Orleans and the Sugar Bowl game with Georgia for the national championship.

"When we got on the plane here to go to Biloxi, [Mississippi,] I remember saying to myself, 'I am not going to do anything for the University of Tennessee until this game is over,'" Majors said. "I will spend this last week enjoying this great team and fully prepare it for this Sugar Bowl game.' And I did. I didn't make any recruiting calls, and we were there in Biloxi and New Orleans for a week."

A Staff Divided

Following the 1978 regular season, Jimmy Johnson—then Pitt's assistant head coach and defensive coordinator—was named the new coach at Oklahoma State University. Johnson, who hired several assistants from Jackie Sherrill's staff to go with him to Stillwater, remained on board for the Panthers' Tangerine Bowl date with North Carolina State.

Offensive tackle Mark May, who was a sophomore that season, noticed that the team's preparation period for the bowl game wasn't up to speed. The Panthers trailed the Wolfpack 17-0 at halftime and lost 30-17.

"Jackie [Sherrill] just went ballistic at halftime," May said. "He read the riot act to those assistant coaches. We heard him screaming at them. After the game, he invited quite a few of the sophomore players up to his hotel suite for a party. He told us, 'The people in this room are the ones who are going to make us great the next two years. This is your team. Whatever happens with this team from this point on is up to you guys. You players are the leaders for this team.'"

Pitt went a combined 22-2—with two bowl victories and top 10 finishes—in 1979 and 1980.

"I think what he did after that bowl game was key," May said. "He empowered us to be leaders. We grew up in a hurry. We took total control of what was going on, on and off the field. That was probably one of the best moves as a head coach he might have made."

Beating Duke There

One of the biggest wins in Pitt basketball history—prior to the Big East—was witnessed by precious few Panther fans. The 13-8 Panthers upset 17-1 and fourth-ranked Duke 71-69 on February 10, 1979, at Cameron Indoor Stadium, snapping the Blue Devils' 22-home game winning streak.

"It was a shock to me," said Panther Sam Clancy, who made the steal and game-winning basket with two seconds remaining. "We just wanted to give them a good game."

Duke, which had lost the NCAA title game to Kentucky the year before, featured Mike Gminski, Eugene Banks, Bob Bender, and Jim Spanarkel, but the Panthers utilized their superior quickness to stay with the Blue Devils. The game was 69-69 with three minutes remaining. Without a shot clock in college basketball at the time, Duke coach Bill Foster decided to take the air out of the ball. In the closing seconds, Clancy intercepted a pass in the lane and took matters into his own hands.

"I wasn't known for my dribbling ability, but I wanted that basket bad," said Clancy, who finished with 23 points and 11 rebounds. "I went the length of the floor and took a short bank shot. It missed, but I got the rebound over Gminski and put it back in."

That victory remains Clancy's favorite.

"That was big time," he said. "That was the best win we had in my four years. I had never played in an atmosphere like that. It was packed, and all those people were wearing blue and white, hollering and screaming. The Duke fans really appreciate good basketball."

And what about the TV?

Dean Billick, Pitt's sports information director, had to choose between the Pitt-Syracuse game earlier in the season, or the Pitt-Duke contest, for a local telecast. He picked the Syracuse game, a 100-74 rout in favor of the Orangemen.

"I made a gigantic error," Billick said.

Billick could be forgiven, for the surprise victory capped a weekend that had Pitt fans giddy. The day before the upset victory, Central Catholic High School quarterback Dan Marino signed a national letter of intent to play at Pitt.

Trocano's Special Motivation

The 1980 football season was especially memorable for Rick Trocano, who had been Pitt's starting quarterback for parts of his first three seasons. One of the program's all-time passing leaders, Trocano relinquished his position to sophomore sensation Dan Marino—a Pittsburgh favorite.

Trocano, however, had no intention of watching his senior season from the sideline.

"I was toying with the idea of playing free safety," Trocano said. "I thought I had the athletic ability and the know how to do it. If I wasn't gonna get a shot to play quarterback, defense might be my best shot to play."

Trocano presented his plan to Jackie Sherrill at the outset of spring practice.

"He asked me if I had ever played safety," Trocano said. "I lied. I told him I had been All-State [Ohio] as a defensive back in high school. Quarterback was actually the only position I had ever played in football."

Trocano's wish was granted, and he found himself starting at free safety for the season opener against Boston College. Five weeks later, Marino injured his knee in the first half of a home game with West Virginia. Trocano, playing quick-change artist, was summoned back to offense to play quarterback and led the Panthers to four touchdowns in the second quarter in the Panthers' 42-14 victory.

The following week, Pitt visited Tennessee—and former coach Johnny Majors. Having a full week of preparation at his customary position, Trocano felt confident going into the game at Neyland Stadium. Tennessee was quarterbacked by Jeff Olszewski, who was from the same general area in Ohio as Trocano. Sherrill wanted to make sure his quarterback was properly motivated.

"Right before the kickoff, Jackie came over to me on the sideline and said, 'You know, when I signed you, John Majors called me to say he signed the better quarterback.' Then he just walked away."

Pitt and Trocano defeated the Vols 30-6.

1980 Panthers Had Star Quality

November 8, 1980, was senior day at Pitt Stadium for Mark May, Hugh Green, Russ Grimm, Rickey Jackson, et al. The Louisville Cardinals were the opponent, and during the walk-through before the game, May noticed that a few Cardinals were making their way—cautiously—toward the Pitt players.

"They were walking rather sheepishly," is how May described it. "Joe Jacoby—who ended up as one of my teammates with the Redskins—and some of his compadres were coming our way. We didn't know what they were thinking. I thought, 'Uh, oh, here we go. There's gonna be a fight, or something.' They asked if they could have some pictures taken with us and get some autographs! This was before the game!"

Louisville actually took a 9-0 lead in the game, but Pitt won 41-23.

"We still laugh about that to this day," May said.

Defensive Front Was the Best

Pitt's 1980 defensive line was probably the best in school history. The five starters—all seniors—were NFL draft picks and made their clubs as rookies. It was a unique blend, with a pair of defensive ends (Hugh Green and Rickey Jackson) from the South and the three interior linemen (Bill Neill, Jerry Boyarsky, and Greg Meisner) from Pennsylvania.

"Other than getting dunked in milk, we were like a big Oreo cookie," Meisner jokes, noting the skin colors of the two components.

Their unique camaraderie was developed early on, during training camp at West Liberty State (West Virginia) College in 1977, following Pitt's national championship season.

"The freshmen were separated from the rest of the other guys in a small locker room," Meisner said. "It was a pretty smelly setup. We scrimmaged the returning players just about every day. That was a real wake-up call for us, but we hung together pretty well. That gave us a lot of confidence right there."

Meisner, who was from New Kensington, Pennsylvania, lived closer to Pitt than any of the linemen.

"With Hugh and Rickey being from the South, we included them in everything," he said. "We'd take them up to my hunting camp and to my mother's house for dinner on Thursday nights. We learned to trust each other."

That spirit carried over to the football field, where the 1980 Panthers led the nation in total defense and rushing defense. For the season, they allowed a per-game average of 69 yards rushing and a paltry 1.6 yards per carry. Pitt held nine of its 12 opponents to single digits. The front five alone accounted for 49 sacks.

"They all had great passion for football," said Foge Fazio, their defensive coordinator. "They were tough guys—mentally and physically. Nothing bothered them. If they were in a situation where their backs were to the wall, it didn't phase them."

"We had to fight to get to the ball to make tackles," Meisner said. "We'd have bets among ourselves—not for money—about how we would hold Joe Morris [Syracuse] or Charlie Wysocki [Maryland] to a certain number of yards."

Their togetherness had a hard, humorous edge as well. During a party at Jackie Sherrill's house, defensive line coach Bob Matey offered Meisner five dollars to eat a night crawler. Meisner collected. At practice and during games, Meisner and Boyarsky would make bear calls to each other at the line of scrimmage.

"It used to echo great inside Pitt Stadium," Meisner said. "It was a lot of fun. We didn't care what people thought."

The Panthers did come to realize what opposing offenses were thinking.

"We would talk to guys on the other team," Meisner said. "We'd say to a guy, 'We'll see you in the backfield.' By the end of the first quarter, there were some offensive linemen who quit."

Meisner attributed much of the success for the team's attitude and performance to Sherrill, Matey, and Fazio.

"With Jackie, the players always came first, and he'd stand up for us," Meisner said. "He always spoke what he felt, which didn't always make some people happy, but we'd have cut our nuts off for him. The compassion that he had for the players rubbed off from the players to each other.

"Foge, that son of a gun could recruit with anybody. All the mothers loved him. He was a good salesman. Bob Matey was our line coach. He wasn't that much older than we were. We'd do anything for him. He would never ask us to do anything for him that he knew couldn't be done. He'd take us to his house and make us tacos for dinner."

Clancy Could Have Been
a College Football Player

Sam Clancy enjoyed a 12-year career as a pro football player in the NFL and USFL but never played a down of football in college. Instead, he became the only player in the school's basketball history to collect both 1,000 points and 1,000 rebounds.

It could have been a different story for the six-foot-six, 245-pound Clancy, who did go out for spring football at Pitt in 1980.

"Looking back, if I had had as much confidence in myself then as [football coach] Jackie Sherrill did, I would have concentrated on football. I really liked Sherrill. I could always depend on him for help. He was one of the best guys around. He would take me into his office and show me film of myself and explain things to me, point out what I was doing wrong and how I could correct it."

Clancy, who had played football at Fifth Avenue High School (later Brashear), did not complete spring practice with the Panthers, opting to concentrate on his basketball career. He later became the defensive line coach for the New Orleans Saints and then the Oakland Raiders.

"I played football in high school for fun, not to get anything out of it," he said. "I did it because a lot of my friends were on the team."

Six Passes, No Completions, One Victory

The opponent was a familiar one and the result was typical, but Pitt's Method of Operation was anything but standard when the Panthers defeated West Virginia 17-0 at Mountaineer Field on October 10, 1981.

The Panthers entered the game 3-0, riding the arm of junior quarterback Dan Marino, who had thrown 13 touchdown passes in the first three games. But the week before, while tossing for six touchdowns in a 42-28 win at South Carolina, Marino sustained a badly bruised shoulder and would miss the showdown in Morgantown.

Enter Danny Daniels, a fourth-year junior—and a new offensive strategy.

"By Wednesday of that week, we knew that I was gonna start," Daniels said. "We knew we weren't gonna throw the ball 40 times, but in no way did we feel that we would throw it only six times."

Daniels had a chaotic week, made only more hectic by teammates and Brackenridge Hall suite residents Jay "J.C." Pelusi and D.J. Cavanaugh.

"The guy who kept me most at ease that week was D.J., Matt Cavanaugh's brother," Daniels said. "He just tortured me. 'You have nothing to be nervous about. It's just your first start, in front of 50,000 people. Don't worry about it.'"

Actually, the Mountaineers—who had to be thinking about Marino in their preparations—dictated that the Panthers keep the ball on the ground.

"West Virginia played a five-two defense, with what we call a 'bubble' on either side of the line," Daniels explained. "That meant their defensive tackle was on the outside shoulder of either [Pitt offensive tackle Jimbo] Covert or [Bill] Fralic, and their nose guard was head up on [center] Emil Boures. That put their linebacker in the bubble, five yards beyond our guard [Ron Sams or Rob Fada]. We planned it where that would be our audible, that I would look either right or left. We were in the I formation, with Wayne DiBartola and Bryan Thomas as the backs. I couldn't believe they were gonna play on the outside of either Covert or Fralic. That was just a matter of those guys pushing the offensive tackle aside, then having a five-yard head start at the linebacker, assuming Emil would handle the nose guard."

"That game was a great opportunity for Danny Daniels and me," said Thomas, Pitt's tailback who had made his first career start in the win at South Carolina. "It was pretty clear that we were going to try and stay on the ground that day. There was a lot at stake in that game. It was West Virginia—a big rival—and both teams were undefeated."

The Panthers stuck to their plan, using Thomas and DiBartola to wear down the Mountaineers, while the defense—with nine starters missing from the great 1980 team the year before—pitched a shutout. Daniels threw six passes, completed none, and had one intercepted, but he took command of a ground attack that featured DiBartola (103 yards) and Thomas (99 yards). The biggest run of the day was a 43-yard touchdown burst by Thomas late in the first half when the game was still scoreless.

"It was a sprint draw," Thomas said. "As I took the ball and went through the line, one of the down linemen had grabbed my helmet or facemask, and I felt my head swivel. I was able to continue my momentum, trying to pull the facemask across my eyes so I could see. I was able to keep my balance enough where I was able to break into the secondary and just sprint to the end zone."

A star had been born. Thomas was Pitt's featured back for the remainder of that season, along with the 1982 campaign. He rushed for 217 yards in a 42-14 win against Florida State the next week in Pittsburgh and had 1,132 yards in 1981.

"It wasn't intentional that we were not gonna throw the ball," Daniels said. "We just thought, 'Okay, if they're in that defense, we'll just run the ball and get five yards every time. What that did, too, was it kept the ball out of West Virginia's hands. They had Oliver Luck at quarterback. They weren't as talented as were going into that game, but we knew it was a big rivalry, that we couldn't afford to take them lightly."

"I just felt that something positive had to happen for me sooner or later," Thomas said. "Danny Daniels and I had come to Pitt together as freshmen in 1978. I'm grateful that Jackie Sherrill had enough faith in us to give us that opportunity. Most young guys, that's all we were looking for."

Marino to Brown

Pitt trailed Georgia 20-17 at the 1982 Sugar Bowl in New Orleans. The Panthers faced a fourth-and-five play at the Bulldogs' 33 with 42 seconds to play. Quarterback Dan Marino conferred with the coaches on the sideline.

"Danny said, 'Coach, we didn't come here to tie the game,'" Jackie Sherrill said. "I knew then that he would get it done."

When play resumed, weary tight end John Brown took his spot in the offensive formation.

"I can't come up with the words to try to explain how exhausted I was at that moment of the game, and I was pretty well condi-

John Brown (left) and Dan Marino celebrate the winning touchdown pass against Georgia in the final moments of the 1982 Sugar Bowl.
Photo courtesy of the University of Pittsburgh Athletic Department

tioned," Brown said. "The last two or three snaps, breaking the huddle I remember thinking, 'Let's end this thing—for better or worse. If we go down, we go down. I'm done. I don't have a play left in me.' Then you go to the huddle and you have another play in you."

The Bulldogs didn't do anything fancy in their attempt to make one final stop.

"We recognized right away that they were in man-to-man coverage," Brown said. "It was easy to tell because they had eight men crowding the line of scrimmage, and three guys across the field."

With Dan Marino at quarterback, all eligible receivers knew what to expect.

"We were always on the same page," Brown said. "Given the structure of our offense and factoring in the type of player Marino was, you always ran your routes in anticipation of getting the ball."

What happened was, arguably, the single most electrifying play in Pitt football history, considering the circumstances. The 10-1 Panthers were trying to redeem themselves following a 48-14 loss to Penn State in the season finale and to register their third straight 11-1 campaign.

Marino hit Brown down the middle for a dramatic game-winning touchdown. Pitt prevailed 24-20.

"The crazy thing about it was they tried to blitz, and they left one-on-one coverage with John Brown down the middle of the field," Marino explained in *Paths of Glory*, Pitt's video highlights tape. "That was kind of a mistake."

"That play was a perfect example of football being the ultimate team sport," Brown said. "There were 11 guys, under the most adverse conditions, totally fatigued, and everybody responded perfectly."

The most impressive part of the play—Marino's perfect pass notwithstanding—was Brown's ability to hold on to the ball after taking a hit from Georgia's Ronnie Harris.

"I never felt a thing," Brown admits. "Something happens to your concentration level that you're concentrating in such a way that's almost out of body. It's the power of the human mind. Those are hits that you feel the next day, maybe even that night, but you don't ever feel it as it's happening."

Not a Bad Deal for Marino's Backup

When Danny Daniels, younger brother of former Pitt quarterback Bill Daniels, followed his heart and signed with the Panthers after the 1977 season, he wasn't thinking about another scholastic quarterback who was a year behind him. A kid named Dan Marino.

"To this day, when people introduce me to someone, they might say, 'He played for Pitt. He backed up Marino.'" Daniels said. "And that's fine. What I say is, 'Who would have beat out Marino?'"

There was never much question about where Daniels would attend college.

"I really wanted to go to Pitt," he said. "I had seen the success that [Johnny] Majors had, and my brother, too. There was a winning tradition at Pitt. Plus, I didn't want to leave home."

Daniels remains philosophical about his experience at Pitt from 1978 to 1981.

"Who can get a free education, go to five different bowl games, letter three years, and say, 'Boy, that was pretty disappointing?' I don't think so. Of course you want to play. That's the competitor in you. But how many people get to have that type of opportunity?"

"Mediocre" Panthers Inherit, Then Leave Eastern Eight

Coach Gale Catlett and his West Virginia basketball team were feeling good about themselves—and with good reason. The Mountaineers had just defeated Pitt 82-77 at the Coliseum in Morgantown on February 24, 1982, before a sellout crowd of 16,704. It was WVU's 23rd straight win, and it completed a regular-season sweep of the Panthers.

After the game, a Pittsburgh writer asked Catlett if Pitt and West Virginia would continue to play in basketball, considering this was the Panthers' final season in the Eastern Eight. School officials had accepted an invitation to join the Big East in 1982-1983.

Catlett couldn't answer for sure, but he did go on to label Pitt's basketball program as "mediocre."

Roy Chipman's Panthers weren't saying "deal." They were looking forward to a chance meeting with West Virginia at Pittsburgh's Civic Arena the first weekend in March.

"We're going to meet them in the finals [of the Eastern Eight Tournament], and when we do, it will be the same as the last two times, right down to the wire," said Clyde Vaughan, Pitt's leading scorer, to reporters afterward.

"I feel very confident leaving here [Morgantown]," Pitt coach Roy Chipman said. "I hope we get another opportunity to play them."

Vaughan and Chipman both proved prophetic. Pitt defeated Rutgers in the semifinals in Pittsburgh, setting up a championship final against WVU. Vaughan was even bolder the night before the third game with the Mountaineers, the league's regular-season champion.

"We're going to beat them tomorrow night," he said. "There's no doubt in my mind it's going to happen."

"I don't know if we will beat them, but we're capable of beating them," Chipman offered.

Vaughan was true to his word, earning tournament Most Valuable Player honors in leading the Panthers past WVU 79-72 in front of a sold-out Civic Arena. The victory gave the Panthers an automatic berth in the NCAA tournament.

"Ironhead" Heyward Was a Kid at Heart

Alex Kramer, Pitt football's chief administrative assistant to five different head coaches, helped arrange visits by Panther players to Pittsburgh's Children's Hospital. The program gave Kramer a unique perspective into the character and personalities of the players.

"Craig Heyward had a lot of child in him," said Kramer. "I remember there was one lad we went to see who had terminal cancer—a very sick adolescent. Craig promised he'd bring him a football the next visit, which he did. Craig had a very big heart. When our time for visiting was over, Craig would often stay behind in the game room and play with some of the kids. It wasn't something he had to do, and he didn't do it out of any sense of obligation. He did it because he genuinely enjoyed doing it. He had fun playing the types of games these kids played. He was a kid himself. He was a 245-pound kid."

The Bill Osborn Story

Bill Osborn played football, basketball, and baseball at Pitt, but if new defensive coordinator John Fox hadn't gone to bat for the youngster in the spring of 1986, Osborn might have been only a *two*-sport Panther.

At the outset of the Panthers' spring drills that year—Mike Gottfried's first season as head coach—Osborn was in Florida with the Pitt baseball team. When Gottfried asked where Osborn was, Fox had to explain the situation.

"Right off the bat, I was in Coach Gottfried's doghouse," Osborn said. "Coach Fox and I had hit it off pretty well, so he talked to Gottfried. [Fox] saved me from getting thrown off the team."

Osborn showed up at his first football practice sporting a sweet tan that didn't impress the head coach.

"Coach Gottfried met with me and told me that I had to run twice as much as the other players to catch up," Osborn said. "I had to do my running at 5:30 in the morning at Pitt Stadium. It was that or get kicked off the team and lose my scholarship."

A defensive back during the spring, Osborn was switched to wide receiver before training camp in August. In between, he contracted mononucleosis. When camp opened, he was buried on the depth chart.

"We had a scrimmage at Jeannette High School," Osborn remembers. "Mike Gottfried was the type of coach who didn't want you to curse or chew [tobacco] or do anything like that on the football field. There was a play where the official ruled I didn't catch the ball. I was ranting and raving. Coach Gottfried used to be right there in the huddle at scrimmages. Well, he didn't like what I was doing. He threw me out of the scrimmage right then and there."

Osborn feared the worst when, later that night when he was exiting the Pitt team lounge just inside Gate 3, Gottfried called to him.

"I thought, 'Oh, great. That's it; I'm gone,'" Osborn said. "He said to me, 'Hey, Bill. You had a good scrimmage. Let's go call your dad and tell him about it.'"

According to Osborn, Gottfried used Osborn's case as an example of why a player should never quit. The Bill Osborn story was a much-repeated tale around the Pitt football program.

"John Congemi would bring a bullhorn into the showers and announce, 'We're on Chapter Eleven of the Bill Osborn story,'" Osborn said.

Congemi's Valor

John Congemi crouched his body and lowered his head while a Syracuse defender approached during the Pitt-Syracuse game November 1, 1986, at the Carrier Dome.

"It took him a little longer to get to me than I thought," Congemi said. "My head kept getting lower, and his head was getting lower. We met and butted heads near the Syracuse sideline. It felt like an enormous flame had gone off inside my back."

Congemi rolled over and saw several SU players and their coach, Dick McPherson.

"Coach McPherson looked at me and said, 'Lay there, Johnny. Don't move. They're on their way.' I couldn't talk or anything. I felt like I'd had the wind knocked out of me."

Unable to get up under his own power, Pitt teammates and medical personnel escorted Congemi to the locker room for X-rays. There was one problem:

"When I went inside, the X-ray machine was down. [Dr.] Freddie Fu and some other medical people were there. They were asking me where it hurt. They were trying to pinpoint it, but everywhere they touched, it hurt. They thought I may have pulled a muscle from my rib cage in the back."

His back was broken, although that wouldn't become known until the following morning in Pittsburgh.

Congemi was fitted with an elastic wrap that ran from his neck to the middle of his back. He managed to walk back to the Pitt sideline on his own.

"Tony Siragusa came up to me and said, 'We need you, John.' I said, 'Well, I'm gonna try.'"

Congemi did return to the game and tossed a touchdown pass to Craig Heyward in the fourth quarter to give the Panthers a lead. The Orangemen came back, however, to take a 24-20 lead late in the game.

"I had to throw a Hail Mary pass that was incomplete. I got hit, and I couldn't get up. Coach McPherson was one of the first ones out there. He said, 'You played one helluva game today. I don't know how you did it.'"

The following morning, Congemi had to call a neighbor to help him get out of bed and dressed. He did, however, manage to drive himself to Presbyterian Hospital, just down the hill from Pitt Stadium.

"When they took the first X-ray, the doctor told me they must have had a bad tape," Congemi said. "He said there was a bad spot on my spine. We'd better do it again. It really hurt to get myself in the position they wanted me for the X-ray, but I did it. Same thing. They said, 'We have to take another one, because you may have broken your back.'"

The third time was conclusive. There had been compression of three vertebrae, with a hairline fracture of the middle one.

"The doctor said, 'Who do we call?'" Congemi said. "I said, 'Well, I have to call Coach Gottfried, because we play Miami next week, and I can't miss that game.'"

He did, of course, and his college career was over. Congemi did dress for the season finale against unbeaten Penn State but could only watch. He finished his career with 6,467 passing yards and 42 touchdowns.

Miller: Big East Freshman of the Year

When celebrated freshman Sean Miller arrived at Pitt in the fall of 1987, he was coming to a basketball program that had shared the Big East regular-season title the year before. He wasn't, however, about to learn the ropes while seated on the bench. Miller and two other true freshman guards—Jason Matthews and Darelle Porter—represented Pitt's backcourt for much of the 1987-1988 campaign.

"I took over [at point guard] fairly early," Miller said.

Pat Cavanaugh, a former walk-on, started the season at the point, but Miller soon became a mainstay in Pitt's formidable line-up, which had plenty of firepower in the frontcourt. Charles Smith, Jerome Lane, Demetreus Gore, and Rod Brookin—who was declared ineligible after the first semester—just needed someone to get them the ball.

"There were a lot of times that year where the only thing I had to do was make the right decision, throw the ball to the right person," Miller said. "The opposing coach, if he had to pick someone to beat them, it would be me."

Miller appreciated his situation that rookie season, when he was named Big East Freshman of the Year.

"I certainly wasn't alone out there," he said. "I was very fortunate. A lot of times, when a freshman point guard comes in and there are a lot of veterans, that makes you look that much better, and that was the case with me my freshman year."

Miller held his own against the best the Big East had to offer, including Georgetown, Syracuse, Villanova, and St. John's.

"The Big East, back then, was as strong as any basketball conference has ever been," he said. "It was amazing competition. The conference was incredible."

Jerome Lane Brought Down the House—and a Backboard

Four minutes and 36 seconds into Pitt's 90-56 win against Providence on January 25, 1988, Jerome Lane took a feed from Sean Miller. The result is a dramatic moment in Pitt's basketball history.

Lane brought down the Fitzgerald Field House backboard with a shattering slam dunk. The game was delayed for 32 minutes while a new backboard—estimated cost $800—could be installed.

"Man, it was unbelievable," Lane told reporters afterward. "I didn't believe it happened. I was just going to try to slam it as hard as I could, make a good impression on the crowd, and get them fired up. I broke the glass, and it was like, 'Yeah!' I mean, everyone was giving me high-fives. I could have broken three more after that."

The partisan Pitt fans couldn't fathom what they'd witnessed.

"The emotion of the moment was a combination of awe and disbelief," wrote Bob Hertzel for *The Pittsburgh Press.*

A photo of Lane's dunk made the front page of the January 26, 1988, *The Pittsburgh Press.* The headline on the front of the sports page read, "Simply Smashing!" Accounts of the game made reference to NBA players such as Darryl Dawkins and Gus Johnson, who had broken backboards in pro games. Interestingly, while playing for the Pittsburgh Condors, Charlie "Helicopter" Hentz broke *two* backboards in an American Basketball Association (ABA) game against the Carolina Cougars on November 6, 1970.

Lane's basket gave Pitt an early 8-5 lead against the Friars, but the game was never close after that. The Panthers went on to win the Big East Conference regular-season championship that year.

Morningstar Rises Above Rupp Arena

Darren Morningstar was convinced that his time had come. Brian Shorter and Bobby Martin had been seniors the year before, and he was Pitt's main big man entering the 1991-1992 season, his final year.

That's what *he* thought. Morningstar split center duty with sophomore Eric Mobley—who was ineligible as a freshman—during the Panthers' opening game win against Manhattan at Fitzgerald Field House in the first round of the Preseason NIT. That meant a trip to Rupp Arena on November 22, 1991, to face Rick Pitino's Kentucky Wildcats, first-round winners against West Virginia.

The Panthers worked out at Rupp Arena the night before the game. Morningstar began the workout running with the blue (first) squad, but coach Paul Evans asked him to switch sides with Mobley.

"In the Manhattan game, [Evans] got on me for a couple things that I thought were minor," Morningstar said. "I didn't play that many minutes. He was riding me at practice the night before the Kentucky game."

Morningstar talked back to Evans at one point, and the coach invited Morningstar to watch the rest of the practice from the sideline.

"I was ready to leave practice," Morningstar said. "We were staying at a hotel next door to Rupp Arena, but Tony Salesi, the trainer, told me to stay where I was, not to leave. I had thought of myself as a pretty good big-game player, but I'd never had the opportunity at Pitt to be the big guy who gets to play most of the game. My first year at Navy, I played a real good game against Iowa early in the season when they were nationally ranked."

Morningstar, who transferred to Pitt from Navy, had no personal connection with Evans, who had been the head coach there before coming to Pittsburgh in 1986. In any event, Morningstar was one frustrated Panther.

"At the hotel before the Kentucky game, I was miserable," he said. "Sean Miller, who was my roommate, calmed me down."

Rather than mope about playing time, Miller suggested that Morningstar concentrate on Kentucky. The two seniors looked through a Kentucky basketball magazine that was part of the hotel's greeting packet.

"Sean was telling me, 'You know, we could get our ass handed to us tomorrow night if we don't come out and play,'" Morningstar said. "The next morning, I was looking at the sports page, and I saw where we were a huge underdog. I'm thinking, 'Gee, Sean's right. If we don't play our best game, with the way Kentucky presses and hounds you the whole game, we could be in real trouble.'"

Kentucky entered the game riding a Rupp Arena winning streak of 22 games. A crowd of 22,555 came to see the Wildcats make it 23. The opening minutes were disastrous; Pitt trailed 11-2 but calmed down quickly.

"Sean was so good at being able to control a game and break the press," Morningstar said.

The Panthers found themselves with a 13-point lead, 43-30, at halftime. Morningstar was having a field day inside.

"I always thought I could run well for a big man, and in that game if you broke the press you kind of knew where to position yourself on the court to take advantage of a fast break. In our half-court offense, Kentucky had a hard time with me because they were so busy pressuring the ball out front. Their press actually played into our hands, because we were able to break it."

Morningstar finished the game with 27 points, making 12 of 16 shots from the floor. He collected 10 rebounds.

"That game they played me man to man, and I thought the guys guarding me were a little soft compared to what we were used to seeing in the Big East," Morningstar explained. "They were guarding me, but my shots weren't as contested as I was used to. Jamal Mashburn was a great player, but he wasn't a center."

Pitt had contributions from everyone in the 85-67 win. Guard Ahmad Shareef scored 21 points. Freshman Orlando Antigua added nine points, eight rebounds, and four blocked shots. Miller, the point guard, orchestrated everything.

"He played a perfect floor game," Pitino said in postgame remarks.

The 18-point win in one of college basketball's most celebrated facilities was a special treat for Pitt's players.

"They have great fans there," Morningstar said. "The aura of being at Kentucky, with Rick Pitino on the sideline and Dick Vitale there doing the game for ESPN made it extra special. It was a big deal. Pitino was from New York, and they already had their travel plans set to go to New York for the next rounds."

Morningstar eventually came to appreciate the guiding hand of his coach, Paul Evans.

"Coach Evans had a great system in place for big guys," he said. "It was called the 'Power Offense,' and it was designed to get the ball inside. That was a huge advantage big guys had playing for Coach Evans. Most programs are guard-oriented, I think."

But what about the harsh words at practice?

"That was his way of making me better," Morningstar said. "He tried to do everything he could to get every bit of ability out of you. A lot of his coaching style was almost reverse psychology."

Gonzalez Was Key to 1997 Success

Walt Harris and his first-edition Panthers surprised more than a few people by winning six games and earning a spot in the 1997 AXA/Equitable Liberty Bowl. The first-year Pitt coach gave fifth-year senior quarterback Pete Gonzalez much of the credit for the better-than-expected results.

"You can't have any kind of winning team if you don't have a good quarterback," Harris said. "The reason we were able to go to a bowl game that first year was because we had a kid [Gonzalez] who came on at quarterback who no one ever dreamed would play, let alone come on and play at the level at which he played. That was it, in a nutshell."

Gonzalez was part of a strong group of seniors who, although not a supplier of talent for the NFL, helped get the Pitt program moving back in the right direction.

"We had a couple of linemen on offense who were pretty good and a couple backs who were good," Harris said. "Defensively, we got our guys in better shape, making a bigger commitment. The talent level was low, and a lot of the better ones were in that [senior] class."

Special Burden for Pitt Stadium Finale

It was the final game at Pitt Stadium. The pomp and circumstance surrounding the event included a nationally televised game against Notre Dame and the appearance of a host of past Pitt football greats. The players knew that in the stands watching their play would be Tony Dorsett, Bill Fralic, Paul Martha, and Craig Heyward—the big names of Pitt football who had built the legacy they were now a part of. As the date of the game—November 13, 1999—approached, the pressure on the team built.

"I asked the staff what they thought I should say to the players about being in the last game at Pitt Stadium," coach Walt Harris remembered. "[Defensive coordinator] Larry Coyer said, 'You can't dodge it. This is a big game, and we have to win it. There is no way we can soft pedal it. This is it. The pressure is on us.'

"We had our seniors there, and I told the lettermen what I had told the team, that it was an obligation for us to play our best game and to coach our best game. I wanted all the former players to have identity, to have ownership of what was going on, and to be involved in what was going on."

But the team did not disappoint the golden boys of Pitt. They delivered a 37-27 win against the Fighting Irish and sent Pitt Stadium out in style.

"Remember the Run"

The starting point of Pitt's dramatic rise to basketball prominence at the beginning of this century can be traced to New York City's Madison Square Garden, where Pitt won on three successive nights to make the finals of the 2001 Big East Tournament.

Pitt had won three of its final four games of the regular season, the only loss being an 80-69 defeat at Syracuse, and coach Ben Howland felt good about his team heading to New York.

"I knew by the way we were preparing and buying in to what we were doing and moving Jaron [Brown] into a more significant role that we were getting there," Howland said.

The Panthers defeated Miami in the opening round, 78-69, setting up a game against Notre Dame, which had beaten the Panthers twice during the regular season. Pitt came out like gangbusters, jumping to a 15-2 lead in the first five minutes and winning the game 66-54.

"We did something we hadn't done all year, which was to double [team] the post every time Troy Murphy got the ball," Howland said. "That was big for us."

Murphy, Notre Dame's six-foot-11 forward who led the Big East in scoring that season, was held to eight points on 2-11 shooting from the floor.

In the semifinals, Isaac Hawkins made one of two free throws in the final seconds of overtime to give Pitt a 55-54 win against Syracuse, another team Pitt was 0-2 against in the regular season. The great run ended with a 79-57 loss to Boston College in the finals, but the Panthers left New York upbeat for a change.

"Ricardo [Greer] was great all the way along," Howland said. "Brandin [Knight], Jaron [Brown], and Julius [Page] all made major contributions, along with Donatas Zavackas and Chad Johnson."

"Remember the Run" was Pitt's slogan for the 2001-2002 season, even though outsiders weren't as optimistic about Howland's third Pitt team.

"I knew we were gonna be good the next year," Howland said. "We were picked sixth out of seven in our division [Big East West], and we ran away with it. No one knew, but us within."

It Was Business as Usual for Jamie Dixon

During the seemingly hectic, tense time following Ben Howland's departure to become head basketball coach at UCLA, the calmest man—one who may have had the most at stake—was Howland's ultimate successor, Jamie Dixon.

"I think a lot of people were surprised, or amazed, at why I was so calm," Dixon said. "But, in my mind, I just went about doing my job here [at Pittsburgh] and doing my best for the university. I just did what I had been doing all along."

Dixon knew that school officials had been courting Wake Forest coach Skip Prosser as a possible successor, but he remained philosophical throughout that period.

"I knew, either way, I was gonna be in a good situation," he said, knowing that Howland was keeping a position open for him in Los Angeles, pending the outcome of Pitt's search. "I felt very comfortable about my situation in that regard, so that probably had a lot to do with it."

Jamie Dixon (background) emerged from Ben Howland's shadow to become Big East Basketball Coach of the Year in 2004.
Photo by Harry Bloomberg

Pitt Back in Grgurich's Good Graces

Twenty-four years after resigning as Pitt's basketball coach in 1980, Tim Grgurich still had not been back to see the Panthers play a game in Pittsburgh, despite repeated invitations from friends, former players, and coaches. He does, however, wish the program well, although he now admits that wasn't always the case.

"It was hard to go back," said Grgurich, who entered Pitt as a freshman basketball player in 1960, and spent his next 20 years there, the last five as head coach.

Believing that Pitt's administration was less than fully committed to big-time basketball, he resigned one day after the 1979-1980 season. As an assistant coach for the NBA's Phoenix Suns, Grgurich says he participates in good-natured arguments with his players when Pitt plays one of their alma maters. He also thought Pitt made a smart decision to hire Jamie Dixon in 2003.

"That was a great move, a smart move," he said.

He had further praise for assistant Barry Rohrssen, who, like Grgurich, spent some time at Nevada-Las Vegas.

"[Rohrssen] is a great recruiter and a helluva coach," Grgurich said. "He's into the players the right kind of way."

That's What Coaches Like to See

Pitt's 28-21 win at undefeated Virginia Tech on November 2, 2002, featured an overpowering running game, a big-play passing attack, and key stands on defense.

"That was our most dominating game in terms of running the ball against a top, top opponent," coach Walt Harris said. "They were undefeated, ranked third in the nation, and it was on the road. That's a very difficult place to play."

The Panthers were down by 14 points twice but didn't deviate from their plan.

"[Running back] Brandon Miree really showed what we always thought he could be," Harris said. "We had some good plans on offense. [Assistant] coach [Tom] Freeman did a really good job, and our guys did a great job blocking. We got stronger as the game went along, and our defense held it together."

Miree, a transfer from Alabama, carried the ball 23 times for 161 yards, including the game-winning touchdown, a 53-yard scamper in the fourth quarter. Quarterback Rod Rutherford connected with Larry Fitzgerald for three scoring passes to cap a memorable victory for Pitt.

"It was probably one of the hardest-fought games we've had," Harris said.

Dream Tandem: Bryant and Fitzgerald

It could have happened, had Antonio Bryant opted to stay at Pitt for his senior season in 2002. Bryant and Fitzgerald could have been on the field at the same time.

"It'd be a great problem to have, and I think any coach would have loved to have been in that situation," said Bill Osborn, the one-time Pitt wide receiver who later became radio color man for Bill Hillgrove. "That combination probably would have rivaled any NFL team, in terms of ability. Now, experience is a different thing."

Osborn, a serious student of the game, had the pleasure of watching both players during their brilliant careers as Panthers. He assessed both:

"In Antonio, you have a guy who is blessed with great quickness," he said. "He was lanky, and he put his body in awkward positions, but still came up with great catches. He has better than average hands, and he's a fierce, fierce competitor. He has a knack for making big plays without shifting gears, so to speak. He has a wiry-type body that bodes well for coming in and out of breaks and catching balls on the fly."

Fitzgerald, who played only two seasons at Pitt, had a different style, but the results were just as remarkable.

"Larry has a big, strong body, and he has supernatural abilities to adjust to the ball," Osborn said. "That ability is unparalleled. He has unbelievable hands. He has more of a quiet confidence, but he's a fierce competitor, too. He expects to make every catch."

And how would an offense attack opposing defenses with such a unique one-two punch?

"If a defense doubled [covered] a receiver, and the quarterback had a grasp of the system, you'd almost be unstoppable," Osborn said. "There would always be someone open."

"I Never Want the Attention to Be Solely on Me"

Larry Fitzgerald had a role model for his signature gesture on a football field—handing the ball back to an official following a touchdown.

"I was a big, big Barry Sanders fan, and he would never make a big fuss out of anything," Fitzgerald said. "To this day, he still shies away from the camera. I wouldn't say I'm as camera-shy as he is, but I never want the attention solely on me, because football is something that's team-oriented. A touchdown is 11 guys working together, executing a play."

Fitzgerald says there's so much that happens on a play that many people don't even realize.

"It's the running back picking up the backside linebacker on the blitz, that allowed the quarterback to throw that fade route to me in the end zone," he explained. "It's the tight end clearing out over the middle. You don't really see or realize that until you're in the film room. There are so many guys who have a hand in making a big play. You can't go out and celebrate like that. I don't feel that I should do that."

That's Scary, Larry

You only thought you'd seen the best of Larry Fitzgerald, the most spectacular catches any collegiate wide receiver could make.

Not so, according to Fitzgerald.

"I make a lot of better catches in practice," Fitzgerald said. "It's never gonna get talked about, but our video production guy has all my practice catches on tape. If you don't believe me, you can go in there and watch."

Fitzgerald: Oh, So Close

Inside a small room of the Yale Club in New York City on December 13, 2003, four outstanding college football players, school officials, sponsors, and fans waited nervously while ESPN broke away to a commercial. Next up: the announcement of the 2003 Heisman Trophy winner.

"When I sat down there, I really felt I had a legitimate opportunity to win the award," Fitzgerald said. "I felt I had put myself in a great position. I didn't play as well as I could have in a few games down the stretch, but nevertheless, I felt I had a great year and was deserving of the award. But, I was extremely excited for Jason White, for having overcome all the adversity he had in his career."

"When I heard 'Jason White,' I remember nodding my head and thinking, 'Yeah, I think we knew it was going to happen this way,'" said E.J. Borghetti, who helped coordinate Fitzgerald's Heisman publicity effort.

Immediately after the announcement, runners-up Fitzgerald, Mississippi's Eli Manning, and Michigan's Chris Perry were to ascend—via elevator—to another room for a separate press briefing.

Borghetti went to the back of the room where the elevators were located. While there, he saw the voting totals flash on a screen. Fitzgerald had fallen 128 votes shy.

"I lost my grasp," Borghetti said. "I said, 'Dammit; it was so close.'"

Borghetti and Fitzgerald rode the elevator alone.

"[Fitzgerald] looked at me and smiled and said, 'That was so close, man.' Then we both laughed about it."

The weekend in New York also was an opportunity for Fitzgerald to make new friends with some of the finest from the college football fraternity.

"I still talk to Eli Manning and to Chris Perry," he said. "The other three candidates were classy, deserving guys."

Morris and the Oakland Zoo

Toree Morris wanted to show his appreciation to the Oakland Zoo, Pitt's student body, during Senior Day ceremonies at the Petersen Events Center on March 6, 2004. Morris, a one-time starting center whose playing time decreased along with the development of Chris Taft, tossed his Big East Championship hat and T-shirt into the crowd.

"I don't know everybody there, but I know the guys who got it started a few years ago when we weren't the best in the Big East," Morris said. "I did that to show them how much I love them."

"We All We Got"

The 2001-2002 Pitt basketball team benefited from the NCAA's newly adopted policy of keeping higher seeded teams close to home for early-round games of the tournament, but that was of no consolation when the 2003-2004 Panthers discovered they were headed to Milwaukee—and a possible second-round game with Wisconsin—for the beginning of tournament play.

Two seasons before, the Panthers defeated Central Connecticut State and California in the first two rounds of the NCAA's in games played at Mellon Arena, just a few miles down Fifth Avenue from the Pitt campus. This time, the Panthers defeated Central Florida in the opening round, setting up a showdown with the University of Wisconsin, 75 miles from the Badgers' campus in Madison.

To demonstrate their united front against what appeared to be a slight—including a No. 3 seed for the tournament—Pitt's players had T-shirts made up with the inscription, "We all we got." The day before the Wisconsin game, coach Jamie Dixon talked about his team's situation.

"I think with every system, it's not going to be perfect, and we don't expect it to be," he said. "You just have to deal with what has been handed to you. We've done that all year long. Whether it's the BCS [Bowl Championship Series] or the NCAA Tournament, it's never going to be perfect."

The Panthers rallied from a 48-44 deficit to defeat the Badgers 59-55 and earned a third straight trip to the Sweet 16.

"We knew coming in it was a road game," Jaron Brown said. "We just stuck together like our T-shirts said: 'We all we got.'"

"We've been in hostile environments before," said point guard Carl Krauser, who made the game-winning shot for the Panthers. "It's just basketball. We just wanted to trust each other, rely on 'We all we got' to get the win."

CHAPTER TWO

TOUGH TIMES

Vote "No" to Rose Bowl

Dark clouds were forming over Pitt's football program in 1937, what turned out to be another national championship season for the Panthers.

On the field, Pitt compiled a 9-0-1 record, marred only by a third straight tie with Fordham, but at season's end, when an invitation for a third consecutive Rose Bowl was extended, Jock Sutherland did something unusual. Emil Narick, a sophomore that season, explains:

"Whenever there was a decision about going to a bowl game, it had always been the decision of the head coach, Jock Sutherland," Narick said. "But after that season, when the invitation was made to go to the Rose Bowl again, Jock didn't make the decision. He said, 'I'm going to leave it to you, the players, to make that decision.

"We met in one of the buildings on campus, maybe Thaw Hall. I'm not sure. There were 33 players there. Some of the players had played there the year before, some two straight years, and they weren't as excited about going back. They had missed the holidays at home and didn't want to have that happen again. I, of course, as a sophomore, had never been to the Rose Bowl, so I was part of the faction that wanted to go. We wanted a chance to go to play in the Rose Bowl. We thought it was unfair not to have that opportunity."

The vote was 17-16 to reject the invitation.

"I'll never forget that," Narick said. "But the players who voted against going were very strong in their feelings. They were pretty bitter about certain things at that time."

"Certain things" involved philosophical differences between Sutherland and the school's hierarchy, both academic and athletics.

"I think the older players on the team sensed from Jock that there must be some problem, because of the fact that he left the vote up to us," Narick said.

"We knew there was something going on because of the way Jock acted, but it wasn't something he talked about," Marshall Goldberg added. "There were rumors going around that the chancellor [John Bowman] was forcing him out. The administration was doing certain things that were going to make life much more difficult. I was very instrumental in [the players] turning down the invitation. To our surprise, Jock was jubilant about our decision not to go to the bowl game because it cost Pitt a lot of money."

The entire affair came to a head following the 1938 season, when the bickering became public knowledge. Angry Pitt students wanted to make a stand in favor of Sutherland.

"At that time I was pretty involved on campus as far as activities and student government," Narick said. "The students were planning to have a meeting at Soldier's and Sailor's Memorial to consider taking some type of action."

Narick pleaded with the students to allow him to approach Sutherland and make the coach aware of what the students were thinking.

"He had an office in the Cathedral of Learning, and I went there and explained to him that the students were considering a strike against Pitt, of walking out, and I just wanted him to know that," Narick recalled. "He said, 'Narick, you go back and tell those students not to do anything. Don't walk out. Don't strike.'"

The students did not strike, but Sutherland walked out, leaving an overall coaching record at Pitt of 111 wins, 20 losses, and 12 ties.

1939 Season: Fun and Disappointment

Jock Sutherland was gone, but Pitt football went on, and the 1939 season was the first for new coach Charley Bowser, who had been an assistant under Sutherland.

The season started on a positive note, a 27-6 victory at Washington.

"We were the first college team to fly by airplane to a game," Emil Narick remembered. "That was quite an experience. It took us two days to get to Seattle. We made stopovers in Chicago; Cheyenne, Wyoming; and Butte, Montana."

What happened after the game was even more exciting for Narick and his teammates.

"Some fella who had won a lot of money betting on the game arranged a party for us," he said. "It was a lot of fun. There was plenty of food, and we danced with some gals. I even corresponded with one of the gals for a short period after that.

"On the way back to Pittsburgh, we stopped again a couple of times, and some of the players took some pictures that were hanging in some of the airport terminals. They were hiding them in their bags and under seats, but when we got to the airport in Pittsburgh, the sheriff was waiting for us. He threatened to arrest the players who had taken the pictures. The players returned everything."

Pitt won its first three games that season, but a 21-13 loss to Duquesne served as an indicator to the veteran Panthers that something was wrong.

"We gradually found ourselves not being as disciplined as we should have been," Narick said. "We were missing what we had been under Jock [Sutherland]. He had us going the right way. Bowser—and I don't mean to be critical of him—but I don't think he had the sense of discipline that should have been imposed on the players as Jock had. As a result, we lost a few games that we shouldn't have. We lost to Penn State [10-0] in the final game. We could almost see ourselves going down. I sensed it. It was hard to really put your finger on it, but things were just different. The beginning of the season, we continued to carry on with the tradition of what we had learned from Jock, but as the season progressed we began losing that."

The 1939 Panthers flew to Seattle to meet Washington in the season opener.
Photo courtesy of the University of Pittsburgh Athletic Department

Another member of the 1939 Panthers felt the same way.

"We felt a great loss [after Sutherland's resignation], said Ernie Bonelli, in the video *Paths of Glory.* "It's not that Charley Bowser coming in didn't do a fairly good job, but he still was not *the* man, Jock Sutherland."

The Red Jerseys

Clark Shaughnessy replaced Charley Bowser following the 1942 football season, and he arrived in Pittsburgh with a slew of innovations—including a drastic change in the team's wardrobe. Blue and gold were out; red and white were in.

"[Shaughnessy] had come to Pitt from Stanford," said Ralph Hammond, who played for the Panthers in 1941 and then in Shaughnessy's first two seasons (1942 and 1943) with Pitt. "Stanford's colors were red and white. His theory was—and this was during the war years—that red jerseys made the team members look bigger."

As Hammond remembers it, the idea went over without any protest from the players or the university-at-large.

"I think the players accepted it, thinking it wasn't a bad idea," Hammond said. "He felt like he was going to turn things around. He had some good ideas. It was a little different than the old single wing offense that had existed around Pitt for so long. He had some good ideas, but he had a hard time getting his plays and his system over to the players."

The college football deck was stacked against the Panthers for much of the 1940s.

"Pitt football was in the doldrums in that era," Hammond said. "We had 4-Fs and students who normally wouldn't have been out for football. The unfortunate part was we played Army [in 1941], with the best team they ever put on the field."

Army beat the Panthers 69-7, as part of a 9-0 season that ended with a No. 1 national ranking at season's end.

"That West Point team, I don't think there will ever be a team that will compare to that," Hammond said. "They had guys who had played ball three or four years, then went away, and came back for West Point. It was kind of a crazy situation, but it existed."

Please Don't Eat the Apples

Pride wasn't the only thing hurting after the Pitt football team lost at Michigan State 53-26 on October 27, 1951. Panther Lou Palatella, a 230-pound tackle, overextended himself on the postgame snack—and wound up extended himself.

"I ate a bunch of apples after the game," Palatella said. "There were apples available in the locker room. I hadn't eaten since that morning. That was on an empty stomach, and it created a real problem."

"On the plane going home, Lou was really in pain," said Alex Kramer, the team's manager. "He was suffering."

When the plane landed in Pittsburgh, Kramer and Joe Schmidt whisked the ailing player to Presbyterian Hospital on the Pitt campus. The diagnosis: an extended stomach.

"They put me to sleep," Palatella remembered. "I woke up 24 hours later, and I felt great."

Marine Panthers Walked Away from a Plane Crash in 1952

It was Labor Day weekend 1952, at the time of the Korean War. Several Pitt football players were stationed at Parris Island Marine Recruit Depot off South Carolina, where they were members of the base team.

"The service football teams at that time were very, very good," said Walt Belich, one of the Pitt men who was there. "They were made up of all college players, sprinkled with some pros."

Also at Parris Island were Pitt gridders Gil Bucci, Nick DeRosa, Bill Sichko, and George Radosevich. The base also included another player with college ties to Pittsburgh—Duquesne University's Leo Elter.

The Pittsburgh-area marines jumped at an opportunity to go home on what was a 71-hour leave. An assistant coach for the football team was co-owner of a twin-engine five-seat Cessna aircraft and offered to have a pilot fly Bielich, Bucci, Elter, and Radosevich to Pittsburgh for $50 round trip. The plane was scheduled to leave Parris Island at 3:30 p.m. on Friday. The then-22-year-old Bielich, who had never flown, was somewhat apprehensive.

"There had been hurricane warnings, and they were battening down the base," Bielich said. "I remember we were all saying, 'Let's get off the ground before they cancel the weekend pass.'"

The plane took off as scheduled and made a brief stopover to refuel in Greensboro, North Carolina. It then departed for Pittsburgh, where it was scheduled to land at the Allegheny County Airport.

"When we got closer to the airport, it became very foggy," Bielich recalled. "Plus, the plane had no instruments, so we couldn't land."

The pilot began diving as he noticed towns below. What he said to his passengers didn't inspire much confidence.

"He asked us, 'Does anybody know where we are?'" Bielich said.

A red light flashed on the control panel, indicating that the fuel supply was low. The pilot, according to Bielich, switched over to emergency fuel, which meant the plane had about 20 minutes of flying time remaining.

"The pilot said, 'Let's head north, and we'll get out of the fog,'" Bielich said. "By this time, I'm thinking, 'We're gonna die.' I didn't want to act like a coward if I'm about to die, so I made peace with myself and tried to go to sleep."

The cabin members sat in silence for the next few minutes until Elter, who was in the co-pilot's seat, yelled, "Look out! We're going down!"

"I woke up just in time as the plane goes into some trees," Bielich said. "We crashed. This wasn't a crash landing. We were down at the bottom of a gulley. There were homes all around the top of the hill. The plane, fortunately, was upright. We skidded up a ditch. Both engines and the wings were torn from the fuselage. The fuselage skidded to a stop. About 10 feet in front of us was a tree, and if we had continued into it, we probably would have been killed."

Everybody was conscious. Bielich bumped his head on the cabin and suffered a brushburn. Radosevich cut his knee. The pilot had a broken nose. Luckily, there was no fire or explosion.

"I always assumed that was because we were probably out of fuel," Bielich said.

The five men managed to crawl from the wreckage and stretched out on the grass. What happened next was reminiscent of a scene from *Night of the Living Dead,* a picture later filmed around Pittsburgh.

"It was like a movie," Bielich said. "All of these people are coming down the hillside to see what happened. It was around 10 o'clock. Some of them were in their pajamas. We said, 'Where are we?' And that's when they told us: 'Meadville.'"

The marines had more than their health and well-being to consider.

"We were what is called 'out of bounds' in the marines," Bielich said. "We were further than we were allowed to go for the weekend. We were hoping that nobody back at the base would hear about this."

The group was taken to a nearby private residence. The state police arrived shortly thereafter to begin their investigation. Coincidentally, one of the young Pennsylvania state troopers on the scene that night was Jim Duratz, later a prominent Pitt athletics booster and benefactor.

In the meantime, someone had alerted the local hospital that there had been a plane crash and to prepare accordingly.

"They [hospital staffers] must have thought it was a big commercial airliner," Bielich said. "Instead, here come these five screwballs—the survivors of the crash—and the entire hospital staff is standing by."

Without any serious injuries, all five went to the state police barracks. Around 2 a.m., an uncle of Gil Bucci, who would then drive to Meadville to pick up the marines, phoned to find out any information. News of the crash had made it to radio reports.

"That's when we all decided we'd better call our families back home to let them know we were okay," Bielich said.

The survivors made it to the Pittsburgh area around sunrise.

"It was a great weekend," Bielich said. "I was a hero. Everywhere I went, people wanted to buy me a drink."

But there was still the business of making it back to Parris Island by Monday morning. The players flew back commercially. There was no grand welcome. In fact, there was hardly any mention of what they'd been through, even though news of the accident had spread across the Eastern seaboard throughout the weekend.

"I'll never forget the first day back at football practice," Bielich said. "Our coach was a colonel—J.T. Hill. He looked at the assistant coach who was part-owner of the plane. Colonel Hill said, 'How much did these men pay to go up to Pittsbugh and come back?' After the assistant coach told him $50, Colonel Hill said to him, 'Well, you know they had to pay their own way to fly back commercially. You owe each one of these men $25!'"

Beano Pushed for Basketball

Beano Cook has become prominent nationally for his opinions and observations about college football, but he is equally passionate when the subject is basketball—especially when he became aggravated by what he felt was a lack of interest an commitment by Pitt's administration during parts of the 1950s and 1960s. An example of his feelings was when the school announced its 1960-1961 basketball schedule.

"I'll never forget," Cook said. "We played Purdue on a Friday night at the Field House, and after the game we flew to Navy to play an afternoon game the next day! When the schedule came out that year, I called [athletic director] Frank Carver. It was around July 4. I always tried to release the schedule two days after the [baseball] All-Star Game. When I saw that schedule, I called Frank and said, 'What are you going to do about it?' He said, 'Nothing. I'm going back out to work in my trees.'"

Cook became even more agitated following a 78-66 loss at Westminster early in Don Hennon's senior year (1958-1959). Again, the telephone rang at Carver's house.

"I called him at home around 11:30 that night and said, 'We just got beat up here by Westminster. What are you gonna do?' He said, 'Nothing. I'm going back to sleep.'"

Cook's overall feeling about the school's attitude toward basketball sounded like the common saying about college football in the South.

"The attitude at Pitt used to be that basketball was something between football seasons," he said.

Buzz

Charles "Buzz" Ridl arrived at Pitt in 1968, charged with reviving what had become a stale, dying basketball program. Mike Paul, who had been a freshman the year before under coach Bob Timmons, recalls how moribund it had become.

"I think everybody knew the program was about as low as it could get," Paul said. "I played as a freshman for [Tim] Grgurich, and we got to scrimmage the varsity every day. You could sense that there just wasn't any excitement about it. The players just didn't seem like they were into it. They were getting pounded all the time. The program was down in almost every aspect. Attendance, excitement... there was none."

Enter Ridl, who had compiled an amazing record of success at tiny Westminster College, including victories against Pitt.

"His reputation was so good that you had to respect him," Paul said. "He was very straightforward and sincere."

Early in Ridl's first season, he dismissed several older players from the team for inappropriate behavior during a road trip to Florida.

"That kind of set the tone that times were changing," Paul said. "I think he certainly got everyone's attention. They went 4-20 that season, but they took their beatings and I guess, became better for it."

The Panther players also had to undergo an extensive learning program under Ridl.

"His system was difficult to learn," Paul said. "The defenses were complex, and some of the offensive schemes were certainly different."

Individual expression was verboten in Ridl's offense. Paul's description of what Ridl wanted from his players might sound shocking to followers of contemporary basketball.

"That was the nice thing about Buzz's system, you didn't have to manufacture your own shot," Paul said. "In fact, you weren't even allowed to do a lot of that. He didn't want you going one on one. He wanted you to be within the flow of the game and the flow of his offense."

Buzz Ridl was Pitt's basketball coach from 1968 to 1975.
Photo courtesy of the University of Pittsburgh Athletic Department

"His system, the way he did it, it was set in stone," Cleve Edwards said. "You had to do this, this and this."

The Night Pitt Held Pistol Pete to 40

Pitt's basketball schedules were upgraded considerably when Buzz Ridl became coach. One of the new opponents the Panthers faced in his first season was LSU, led by scoring whiz Pistol Pete Maravich.

Billy Downes was the Panther guard who had the unenviable task of guarding Maravich on January 31, 1969.

"We used to kid Bill about what a great job he did holding Maravich below his scoring average," said Mike Paul, a redshirt member of the team in Ridl's first season.

Maravich did score 40 points, on 13 of 34 shots from the floor and 14 of 18 free throws. He also had 11 assists. He had been averaging 44 points per game.

"It was certainly a thrill playing against him," Downes said. "I've gotten a lot of mileage out of that over he years, telling people I held him below his average."

Maravich was the rage of college basketball then, and Downes recalls a few of the particulars.

"He wore those dirty, floppy socks," he said. "They even had holes in them up near the tops. The elastic was completely gone, but it didn't slow him down. They just blew us away [120-79], so the showmanship he displayed really came out. A couple times he came down—just one or two steps beyond midcourt, and let fly with two-handed set shots—swish!"

Downes also angered the Baton Rouge crowd because of a brief struggle with its hero.

"We were fighting for a loose ball, and we both went down," Downes said. "He got up holding his hand, shaking it like it was hurt. The crowd got on me for the rest of the game. You'd have thought I had hurt the king."

The Panther committed 23 turnovers in the first half alone and trailed 67-34 at halftime. There were several blowout losses during that 4-20 season, one of only two 20-loss seasons in Pitt history.

"It's very easy to forget a lot about that season," Downes said.

It ended with a humiliating 68-64 loss at nearby Carnegie Mellon, just down the street from the Pitt campus.

"That was a fitting end to a losing season," Downes said.

Pitt Stadium Barracks for You Guys

Dave Hart remembers what it was like when he and his new football coaching staff arrived in Pittsburgh following the dismissal of John Michelosen in 1965.

"We had been at Navy and, before that, Kentucky, where they had some pretty first-class things," Hart said. "When I came to Pitt, I went to [A.D.] Frank Carver and asked if we could have some place to live until our families could come and get situated. He said, 'No, you'll stay at the [Pitt] Stadium.' We lived in one room. We rented cots, which we had to pay for, and we were all in one room. We had metal lockers that [assistant athletic director] Walt Cummins brought in for us to use. That's where we stayed until our families arrived. We were there through spring practice."

Divine Pep Talk Didn't Help

Following back-to-back 1-9 seasons in 1966 and 1967, it was time for Pitt's football program to step it up. "The Year the Panther Begins to Growl" was the adopted battle cry for the 1968 campaign.

Seeking another form of inspiration, Pitt coach Dave Hart brought in evangelist Billy Graham to address the team during the week leading up to the season opener at UCLA.

"Maybe [Hart] thought it would bring divine intervention," quarterback Dave Havern said. "It was interesting, though. He was real dynamic. You thought you were listening to Charlton Heston. He and Coach Hart had twin personalities. I thought they were twins, except for their hairstyles."

UCLA throttled the Panthers 63-7. Pitt finished the season 1-9.

Losing Took Its Toll

Heinz Field and the University of Pittsburgh Medical Center's Sports Performance Complex give the Panthers a magnificent array of first-class facilities. Yes, Pitt football's come a long way, baby.

Dave Havern can remember the days in the late 1960s when coach Dave Hart and several volunteers had to paint (yes, literally) the locker room at Pitt Stadium.

Hart's three-year term as Pitt's coach produced a 3-27 record. It was especially galling to Havern, because he genuinely believed Hart was a man who had a proper vision for the program. Executing it was the problem.

"If he had been given a few more years, I really believe that he would have turned it around," said Havern, who played his first varsity season in 1968 for Hart, and his final two years for new coach Carl DePasqua. "Believe me, there are some guys who played on those teams who are laughing their butts off at what I just said, but I honestly think he could have gotten this program moving in the right direction."

Havern recalls Pitt's football facilities back then.

"The locker room at Pitt Stadium, my gosh, it was like being in the catacombs," he said. "It was very dark and bland. Our weight room was a single universal machine sitting in the middle of the locker room. That was our weight program. Okay, it was a spartan atmosphere, but I didn't hear talk from players about the facilities, one way or the other."

The grass surface at Pitt Stadium—where the NFL's Pittsburgh Steelers also played their home games—forced the Panthers, at times late in the fall, to practice *across* the field in an area *behind* the end zone, or on an 80-yard grass field near where Sutherland Hall was eventually built.

*Dave Havern attempts a pass against UCLA in the 1970 season
opener, the first game on artificial turf at Pitt Stadium.*
Photo courtesy of the University of Pittsburgh Athletic Department

The players did have some complaints, and their frustrations
mounted with the losses.

"Most of the complaints were about some assistant coaches,"
Havern said. "You know, 'This guy's a jerk,' or 'I'll never play as long
as that guy's here.'"

If the facilities were poor, the off-season conditioning program
was even more primitive.

"Back then it was more of an aerobics and quickness thing," he said. "It wasn't so much about strength."

Some players invented their own training routines.

"I used to go to the lower level at Trees Hall and throw footballs at the archery targets," Havern said. "I also used to run the entire length of the steps to the top floor of the Cathedral of Learning."

But all the sweat and toil failed to pay any dividends on the field for Hart, whose staff included Leeman Bennett, Dick Bestwick, Frank Cignetti, and Bill Lewis, all future head coaches.

"All the losing took its toll on the players," Havern said. "It was especially tough on the seniors in Coach Hart's last year [1968]. I remember the Penn State game, Coach Hart's last game. One of the starting offensive linemen, a senior, came up to me before the game and said, 'If anybody gets you today, it was my guy, 'cause I ain't blocking anyone. I'm out of here.'"

The 65-9 loss to Penn State was the final blow to Hart's program and led to one of the strangest—yet largely forgotten—string of events in Pitt football history.

"Frank Kush Named Pitt Coach"

That banner headline greeted readers of *The Pittsburgh Press* on Sunday, January 5, 1969. Frank Kush, the successful coach at Arizona State and a product of Windber, Pennsylvania, had agreed to return to his home state and coach the Panthers.

But Dean Billick, then Pitt's sports information director, remembered how the announcement of Kush's hiring was made not by his office but by Pitt's public information wing.

"I was never brought in on it," Billick said. "I received a call from a sportswriter who said, 'Congratulations, you have a new coach.' And I said, 'What?'"

That was only the first of a few oddities when it came to the

1969 head-coaching search. After the announcement Kush seemed eager and ready for the task.

"My biggest job at Pitt will be to change the attitude of the fans from losing to winning," Kush told reporters.

But the first attitude adjustment belonged to Kush. Several days after accepting the job, he changed his mind, opting to remain at Arizona State.

Pitt officials had courted several other high-profile coaches at the time but came up empty. Wyoming's Lloyd Eaton and Oregon State's Dee Andros (nicknamed "The Great Pumpkin") were among the candidates interviewed before the school finally turned to one of its own, former player and assistant coach Carl DePasqua.

During the drawn-out search, one publication ran an article with the title, "Doesn't Anyone Here Want This Football Job?"

"Pitt was the brunt of a lot of jokes then," Billick said.

"Take It Easy, Hyde!"

Bob Medwid had an up-and-down career as one of Pitt's quarterbacks during the latter part of Carl DePasqua's tenure. The downs were magnified by a series of injuries, including a broken collarbone sustained in a win against Syracuse in 1971. He suffered a cracked rib during a loss at Air Force the following year. But those injuries, felt during the heat of game action, were routine compared to what happened to Medwid several weeks after that Air Force game.

"We were playing Notre Dame there, and we were playing them tough," Medwid said, "and [defensive tackle] Glenn Hyde blocked a punt and came jumping over to the sideline. He gave me a big bear hug and finished off the rib. I remember DePasqua telling me to go in, and I couldn't even breathe. He said, 'Dammit, you haven't even played yet.' And I said this maniac Hyde just bear-hugged me to near-death."

The Panthers lost 42-16.

How "A Major Change in Pitt Football" Happened

A hot tip from a once-fired coach, a clandestine search involving several boosters, and a substantial cash reserve combined to lure Johnny Majors to Pittsburgh after the 1972 football season.

Early that fall, it became painfully obvious that the Panthers were headed for another losing record under coach Carl DePasqua, then in his fourth year. The decision to make a coaching change, coordinated by Pitt chancellor Wesley Posvar and athletic director Cas Myslinski, was made several weeks into the season. The search for a new coach would begin almost immediately, although Posvar was unaware of its specifics at the beginning.

Four years earlier, Myslinski—in his first weeks on the job—had been scorned repeatedly in his attempt to hire a "name" coach for the Panthers. This time, Myslinski asked several Pitt alumni, all founding members of the Pitt Golden Panthers booster club, for help. The three—businessman C.R. "Bob" Miller, attorney Sam Sciullo, and auto magnate Bill Baierl—were called together by Myslinski to formulate a strategy to find a new coach. Miller, who would play the most prominent role in the search, placed a call to a good friend, former Pitt coach Dave Hart, seeking recommendations for a successor to DePasqua.

"Myslinski had become gun shy, particularly after the Kush affair," Miller said.

"There weren't any headhunters back then to find the most talented people," Hart said. "[The Pitt administrators] didn't want to be embarrassed again. They didn't know which way to turn."

Hart gave Miller three names: Frank Kush; Homer Rice, then the director of athletics at North Carolina who later coached the Cincinnati Bengals; and 37-year-old Johnny Majors, who had turned around Iowa State's football program. As it evolved, the search focused almost entirely on Majors.

"I called Majors, at Miller's request," said Hart, who eventually became the athletic director at both Louisville and Missouri and then the commissioner of the Southern Conference. "I said, 'John, listen to me. If anything is ripe, Pitt is right now, because they're either going to drop the sport or improve it until it's right."

Hart also told Majors that he should expect to hear from one of the Pitt boosters.

"I knew Dave Hart," Majors said. "We talked. Bob Miller and I talked the most. I had made plans to leave Iowa State, if I could. I loved Iowa State, and I loved the Midwest, but it was very, very unlikely that you could win a national championship there. That, plus the fact that the athletic director [there] and I just weren't on the same page."

Majors decided to have his brother, Joe, who was an attorney, take a secret trip to Pittsburgh to see if the opportunity was worth pursuing. John Majors remembers:

"I told him, 'Joe, if you'll go visit with the Pittsburgh people and see what they're like, what's going on, I'll get you a plane ticket.'"

John Majors, the eldest of the Majors children, knew he could believe whatever information his younger brother brought back.

Joe Majors traveled to Pittsburgh to watch the Panthers play. Myslinski, Miller, and Sciullo met him at the airport, where Myslinski kept his distance from the others. They took Majors to the Webster Hall Hotel in Oakland, where he was registered under an assumed name, Mason. At the football game, he sat in a private box adjacent to the press box. While there, he met Posvar and one of his aides, Bernie Kobosky.

"Joe was there under the ruse of being an adviser as far as what the Pitt people should do about getting a coach," John Majors said. "Posvar, according to what I know, did not know that he was John Majors's brother. Cas was very secretive. My name never came out in the papers there until right around the time I took the job."

Joe Majors flew to Iowa to check in with his older brother. They sat in John's house late one night and talked until the early hours of the next morning.

"Joe said, 'John, they're ready to make a move,'" John Majors said. "'They want to get there, but they don't know how to do it. You're the person who can get them there.' That's how much confidence he had in his big brother."

Majors, who had lived and coached in college towns, was skeptical about Pitt's urban setting.

"I told Joe, 'Joe, I don't think I want to live in a city,'" John recalled. "But I said, 'What's Pittsburgh like?' Joe told me, 'John, in November, the drive from the airport to downtown Pittsburgh isn't very impressive. But, John, it's the place for you. You need to go talk to them.'"

Miller was wishing and hoping the same thing.

"Bob Miller kept calling me," Majors said. "He's a great talker. He's such a charmer on the phone. We would usually talk later in the week—Wednesday or Thursday night. If it hadn't been for Bob Miller's charm, I never would have visited Pittsburgh."

"My telephone bills during those months were hundreds of dollars," Miller said.

As it turned out, if Majors wouldn't visit Pittsburgh, Pittsburgh would visit Majors. The day that Iowa State's football team was scheduled to leave for its regular-season finale at Oklahoma State, Myslinski and Miller flew to Iowa and met with John Majors at a hotel near the Des Moines airport.

"They were the first people I interviewed with that year," said Majors, who also was being courted by SMU, Purdue, Michigan State, and Kentucky. Majors, Barry Switzer, and Lee Corso all interviewed for the MSU job that went to Dennis Stolz.

Majors finally agreed to visit Pittsburgh in the weeks prior to ISU's Liberty Bowl game against Georgia Tech. This time, Myslinski was more visible, meeting Majors at Greater Pitt and taking him straight to Pitt Stadium in the dark of night. Majors wasn't exactly impressed.

"The locker room was very dank, dark and not very well kept," said Majors, who had been offered the Kentucky job the night before flying to Pittsburgh. ("I knew that, historically, Kentucky couldn't beat Tennessee, and I didn't want to go back to my area and get my ass beat by my alma mater.")

The next day, Myslinski took Majors to the Field Club in Fox Chapel, where he was introduced to WTAE TV executive John Conomikes. Also at the Field Club that day, but not part of the session with Majors, was Pitt booster Ed Ifft, who would become one of Majors's closest friends in Pittsburgh. Majors also paid a visit to the Posvar residence, where he met with Pitt's chancellor. Majors was impressed by Pitt's campus.

"I had never seen a college campus quite like Pitt's, with the unique architecture of the buildings," he said.

Finally, in Memphis for the Liberty Bowl, Majors sought counsel from a football coaching giant who was in town to work the television broadcast of the game. He met privately with Bud Wilkinson.

"[Wilkinson] told me, 'John, I think you should consider the Pitt job very seriously,'" Majors said. "'They go way back to a great tradition, and there are a lot of good football players in that area.'"

There was another man monitoring Majors in Memphis that weekend.

"Cas [Myslinski] came to town, unannounced," Majors said. "He wanted to be close at hand in case anything happened." The Purdue job remained a strong possibility.

Saturday, December 16, 1972, was a cold, gray day in Pittsburgh. That afternoon, Pitt's basketball team lost to Wittenberg before a crowd of 1,009 at the Field House. Sam Sciullo, an ardent Panther basketball supporter, was in need of good news. It came that night at home, in a phone call from Myslinski.

"Cas told me, 'We [Pitt and Majors] have a deal,'" Sciullo said. "'We shook hands on it.'"

Georgia Tech beat Iowa State 31-30 in the Liberty Bowl two nights later.

"I told the squad in the locker room after the game that I was going to Pittsburgh," Majors said.

Another crucial factor that influenced Majors's thinking was the administration's decision—spearheaded by Posvar—to dissolve the Big Four agreement that mandated the number of football scholarships Pitt, Penn State, West Virginia, and Syracuse could give. It also banned redshirting for non-medical reasons.

Then there was the money. The Bellefield Educational Trust Fund, later known as the Panther Foundation, was Pitt's emergency supply for a rainy day, although that wasn't actually its purpose.

"That money was not to be used for anything except graduate school for the athletes," Miller said. "They weren't grants, but loans, that were to be paid back."

Instead, much of the money paid for all the scholarships the Pitt coaches distributed in Majors's first recruiting effort. It also helped pay coaches' salaries, as well as upgrades to Pitt Stadium. The Bellefield Educational Trust Fund, it can be said, bankrolled The Major Change in Pitt Football.

"That's what funded it," Baierl said. "Without that commitment, Cas [Myslinski] would have been stuck. Who would he have hired?"

How Low Can You Go?

Bill Hillgrove has been through numerous peaks and valleys during his years as radio voice of Pitt football and basketball, but he recalls two football games that were good indicators that the program had sunk about as low as possible.

The first was a 27-22 loss to Northwestern before a crowd of 18,557 at Pitt Stadium on September 30, 1972. (At the same time the Pitt-Northwestern game was being played at Pitt Stadium, a few miles across town at Three Rivers Stadium, the defending World Champion Pittsburgh Pirates were hosting the New York Mets, the game in which Roberto Clemente collected his 3,000th hit. The attendance at the baseball game was 12,117.)

"I was the color man to Ed Conway that year, and I pretty much said that we just weren't competitive," Hillgrove said. "They had a fullback named Jim Trimble, and they just ran over us like we weren't there. I said, 'This team is not competitive.' I hated to say it, but it was the truth. That was the low."

But was it?

John Majors's second four-year stint (1993-1996) at Pitt didn't produce anywhere near the results as his first tour. Included in his final season was a 72-0 loss at Ohio State on September 21, 1996. The Buckeyes scored on their first 10 possessions.

"I felt bad for Billy Osborn that day," Hillgrove said. "As the color man, he was left with nothing to say during the second half of that game because there was nothing left to analyze."

After the game, sports information director Ron Wahl had the unpleasant task of taking Majors to the interview room to meet with the media.

"It was about a hundred degrees there, a real nasty day," Wahl said. "For the postgame press conference, [Ohio State] put us in some stupid auxiliary locker room where it was even hotter. It was just a horrible situation, all the way around."

Another man with an interesting perspective that day was the Buckeyes' quarterbacks coach, Walt Harris. Years later, he recalled Pitt's apparent lack of preparation that day in Columbus.

"[The Pitt coaches] didn't give their players a chance to win," Harris said. "Their deployment on defense was very poor. They had a quarterback who looked like he wasn't very good. They had a good punter. It didn't look like there were very many athletes on the field. They were physical when we played them in '95 [a 54-14 Ohio State win], but the next year they weren't."

Pitt's Un-Magnificent Seven

The Pittsburgh Press headline put it this way: "Pitt's Un-Magnificent Seven Makes Dry Run."

Coach Tim Grgurich was only 33 during his rookie season (1975-1976) as Pitt's basketball coach. He suspended seven players—including four starters—from playing in the Panthers' 60-56 loss at Cleveland State on December 30, 1975.

"I would have done the same thing if we were playing UCLA for the national championship or if we were 8-0," Grgurich told reporters after the game.

In reality, the Panthers were 2-6, and the first-year coach, after consulting with the offenders (including first-stringers Larry Harris, Frank Boyd, Willie Kelly, and Ralph McClelland) decided not to take the players to Cleveland because of a rules violation. The players had been drinking during a road trip to Florida earlier that month and came down with what they preferred to call the "Brew Flu."

Pitt's starting lineup that night consisted of six-foot-one Pete Strickland and five-foot-nine walk-on Dominic Berardinelli in the backcourt, six-foot-five Terry Knight at center, six-foot-three Scott Nedrow and six-foot Tom Richards at the forward positions. Two more walk-ons, Paul Kochka and Jim Windbush, filled out the bench.

"That sorry group was the Pitt basketball team that lost to Cleveland State, 60-56, here last night, and if you didn't know Pitt had played in two straight postseason tournaments, you wouldn't have believed it," Jeff Samuels wrote in *The Press*.

"When we ran out on the floor, there was almost a complete hush from the crowd," said Richards, the lone senior in the lineup. "It was like they were thinking, 'Is that it? Is that your team?' People were just looking at us, almost in disbelief. It's hilarious to think about it now, but it wasn't funny at the time."

The undermanned Panthers held their own, leading by as many as seven points in the first half before foul problems arose later. Three Pitt players were disqualified on fouls, leaving the visitors in the absurd position of playing the final 1:35 with only four players on the court. The shortage of bodies forced a five-second call against Nedrow in the final minute, when Pitt trailed by one, 55-54.

"I didn't know what to do," Nedrow told the press. "We don't practice with four guys. I looked to make a pass, and nobody was there."

Almost 30 years later, Richards refused to criticize his coach for what he did that night.

"Gurg had some qualities that I really respect," Richards said. "He always protected his kids, almost to a fault. He was so loyal. If he felt he had to administer some discipline, that's what he did. I still consider him one of my closest friends, and I would always be loyal to him, because that's the way he was."

6-21

Few could have predicted it, least of all the head coach and his players, but the 1976-1977 basketball season—Tim Grgurich's second at Pitt—produced more losses than any Pitt team before or through 2004.

In Buzz Ridl's last season at Pitt in 1974-1975, the Panthers finished with an 18-11 record and a berth in the National Invitation Tournament (NIT). That team featured a pair of junior stars, point guard Tom Richards and guard-forward Keith Starr, plus freshman center Mel Bennett. Those three could have formed an excellent nucleus for Grgurich's first team, but it wasn't to be. Bennett declared hardship immediately and was a first-round draft choice of the ABA's Virginia Squires. Richards broke his shooting wrist two weeks before the season and was still feeling the pain two months into it. The final setback occurred in Pitt's only exhibition game when Starr went down with a serous knee injury and played only a few minutes in one game that year. Still, faced with all that adversity, the Panthers went 12-15.

"I thought, that first year, Gurg got everything he possibly could have out of that team," said Larry Harris, Pitt's prolific leading scorer in Grgurich's first three seasons.

Pitt was a program in dire need of a talent haul, and Grgurich signed four projected blue-chippers in power forward Michael Rice, center Ed Scheuermann, guard Nathan "Sonny" Lewis, and junior-college point guard David Washington. Grgurich exulted in his efforts and made bold predictions about what his second Pitt team might accomplish, even though the Panthers had few proven veterans returning.

"Before the season, Gurg was talking about Top 20 and this, that and the other, but it turned out to be a major disaster," said Scheuermann, the only member of the recruiting class who made it to the proper end of his career at Pitt. "It was tough. It was certainly something we didn't expect."

There were other factors.

"Terry Knight hurt his knee before the season and had to be redshirted," Harris said. "He would have been another guy, another scorer, coming back. The way it was, we usually had two or three freshmen in the lineup running into each other."

The early results wiped out much of the good work the Panthers had done the year before.

"Toward the end of that [1975-1976] season, I thought we started to gain some momentum," Harris said. "But all the air went out of the balloon. All the momentum we had going, went out."

The players noticed the effect the long, awful season had on their young head coach.

"Gurg is a guy who is really caring, so in that context that season really wore on him," Harris said. "It was tough to go through. I think we all were pretty happy when that season was over."

Before it ended, however, Harris provided one very bright moment when he hit a last-second shot from deep in the corner to give the Panthers a 65-64 win against national power Cincinnati. He led the Panthers with 31 points that night, and was Pitt's go-to guy, a role he accepted.

"That was just the way it was for me," Harris said. "There wasn't anybody with enough experience—other than me—to be able to handle that."

"That Was a Tough, Tough Loss"

A 36-22 loss at Florida State on October 11, 1980, prevented Pitt from adding another national title to its football resume. Instead, the Panthers settled for No. 2 in both wire service polls. The first ever *New York Times* computer rankings did have Pitt No. 1 at season's end.

The 1980 Panthers were caught off guard by the Doak Cambell Stadium revelry, says one prominent player.

"This was a little before Florida State became what you think of them as today," Mark May said. "It was one of the first night games

Clyde Vaughan talks basketball—
and comedy—with Rodney Dangerfield.
Photo courtesy of the University of Pittsburgh Athletic Department

Vaughan was named second-team All-Eastern Eight as a sophomore and third-team All-Big East as a junior.

"People were saying, 'Clyde Vaughan won't be able to do the same things in the Big East that he did in the Eastern Eight,'" Vaughan said. "But I think I finally earned the respect of the coaches. They knew. They saw what I could do. I also knew by the way they set up their defenses to stop me. They knew I could play."

"He wasn't a flashy type of player," Smith said. "He'd just score his 20 points and get nine or 10 rebounds a game. He was only six foot four, six foot five, tops. We never felt he received the proper recognition, either from the media or the coaches."

that we played away. Then, that guy on the horse came out, a
lowered the lights. We didn't know anything about that ritu
Indian came out and threw that spear in the middle of the fi
their fans go absolutely crazy. From that point on, it was an
dating thing. Are we gonna get out of here alive?"

Pitt quarterback Dan Marino, a sophomore, threw
yards and a pair of touchdowns but was affected by the cro

"I had never experienced the type of noise we were u
that game," he said a couple years later. "Although I had
dealing with it then, the experience made me a better quar

The Panthers shot themselves in the foot with seven t
The Seminoles had none. Punter Rohn Stark kept Pitt back
night with his booming kicks, while placekicker Bill Cape
five field goals.

"That was a tough, tough loss," Pitt coach Jackie She

Two Guys Who Get No Respec

Clyde Vaughan led the Eastern Eight in scoring as a s
(1981-1982), then topped The Big East in that same ca
following year, but failed to make first-team All-Confere
time. Kimball Smith, then Pitt's basketball sports informa
tor, found a unique way to illustrate Vaughan's status.

"Rodney Dangerfield was scheduled to appear in Pi
the Stanley Theater," Smith said. "I thought it might be
if we could get him to pose for a picture with Clyde. C
getting any respect, and that was Dangerfield's routine."

Smith knew an operations man at the Stanley who h
be a Pitt fan. He contacted Dangerfield's agent, who wa
the idea. The picture went off without a hitch, even if I
wasn't too hip on Vaughan—or basketball.

"[Dangerfield] was cordial," Smith said. "He asked
tions about Clyde. He wasn't familiar with him. He'd ne
him. He was not a basketball fan, obviously."

Barry Goheen

Barry Goheen's late-game heroics in a second-round game of the 1988 NCAA Midwest Regional left basketball fans dancing in Nashville, but crying—and outraged—in Pittsburgh.

The 1987-1988 Panthers might have been the most talented team in school history. They won the Big East regular-season title by defeating Syracuse at the Carrier Dome in the final game. Although they were upset by Villanova in the Big East Tournament, the Panthers quickly set their sights on the NCAA Tournament, where they easily disposed of Eastern Michigan in the first round at Lincoln, Nebraska. They expected to do the same to Vanderbilt in the next round. If not for Goheen, the Panthers would have been preparing for a Sweet 16 game against Kansas, that year's eventual national champion.

With Pitt leading by four late in the game, Goheen shot a three-pointer to draw Vandy to within one point. Pitt's Charles Smith hit two free throws to increase the lead to three. Time was called.

"There are a lot of different ways to play that scenario," said Sean Miller, diplomatically, many years later. "The point is Barry Goheen had to make two dramatic three-point baskets, both off the dribble. If he shot those 10 times, with no defense, he might make two or three, at best. But he did a great job."

Many observers thought Pitt should have fouled Goheen, but Goheen wasn't even considering that possibility.

"There were four seconds left," Goheen said. "You're thinking, 'Get the ball to somebody and get the best possible shot.'"

That somebody was himself. He took the ball—and Pitt's fate—into his own hands. He had a clear path to his favorite shooting spot and sent the game into overtime 64-64, with a three-pointer at the horn.

"What was unobstructed was my path to that point on the court," he remembered. "I dribbled straight down the court as far as

I could go, in about three and a half seconds, to make sure I got the shot off before the buzzer. There were players standing there with their arms up. It wasn't vigorously contested. There were defenders there; it wasn't just a wide-open shot."

Goheen, a junior that year, had a track record of hitting dramatic shots in the final seconds.

"In that situation, you want to go down and get the best on-balance, pure shot that you could get," he said. "I wasn't thinking about them fouling me, or them trying to foul me, or me drawing a foul. It was pure concentration."

That concentration led to one of the most bitter defeats in Pitt basketball history, a 70-64 overtime setback. Ironically, Vanderbilt was not at full strength for the extra period.

"We beat them in overtime without our best player, [center] Will Perdue," Goheen said. "He fouled out right before the end of regulation."

"The crowd gave Perdue a standing ovation when he fouled out," Miller said. "That would have been his last game in college. That's how in the bag the game seemed to be. It goes to show—you have to finish a game off. Strange things can happen at the end."

The Panthers were a victim of March Madness.

"Every NCAA Tournament seems to have a game like that," Miller said. "Unfortunately, we were on the wrong end of it."

The Vanderbilt Aftermath

Author John Feinstein was preparing to head to the Pitt locker room. *Pittsburgh Post-Gazette* writer Steve Halvonik sat along press row, considering strategy. Larry Eldridge, Pitt's publicist, crouched behind Tommy Heinsohn, who was providing color commentary for the CBS telecast of the Pitt-Vanderbilt NCAA Midwest Regional basketball game at Lincoln, Nebraska, on March 20, 1988. Eldridge needed to find out which member of the victorious Panthers CBS wanted to interview afterward. Barry Goheen, meanwhile, rewrote the script.

Goheen's three-point shot at the buzzer tied the game, sending it into overtime, where the Commodores prevailed 80-74. Pitt's season was over in stunning fashion. The Panthers, whose roster included seniors Charles Smith and Demetreus Gore, along with junior Jerome Lane and an impressive group of freshman guards, trudged off the court.

"That starting lineup was the most talented one I ever played against in college," Goheen said. "It's not even close."

"[Author] John Feinstein had been granted special access to follow several coaches throughout that season, in preparation for a book he was writing about college hoops that season," Eldridge said. "[Pitt coach] Paul Evans and Feinstein had known each other pretty well since Paul had been at Navy, and Feinstein was with *The Washington Post*. Paul liked him."

Dejectedly, the Panthers entered the locker room. Feinstein started to enter, but was stopped by a security official.

"An NCAA guy did try to stop me, but Paul Evans basically said, 'Hey, he's with us. Get out of the way,'" Feinstein said.

Feinstein was the only writer inside the locker room.

"He witnessed some of the acrimony that happened in the locker room, which was okay because he had access, as granted by Paul," Eldridge said.

"Paul tried to be upbeat, saying to the freshmen, 'You had a great year,'" Feinstein said. "But it was an upset locker room. You lose an NCAA Tournament game that way, there are bound to be frayed tempers. There was a sense of disbelief that they had lost the game. I don't think they thought that Vanderbilt could beat them. And, essentially, they had them beat."

The big question on the minds of fans and reporters had to do with Pitt's strategy in the final sequence of regulation. The players, however, did not broach the subject—initially.

"I don't think any of the kids raised the issue of whether they should have fouled," Feinstein said. "I know it came up in the press conference. When the locker room opened, some of the kids questioned some of the strategy."

"When Feinstein came out of the locker room, he proceeded to tell the reporters some of the stuff that had happened inside," Eldridge said.

"Feinstein tipped us off to the fact that there had been dissension in the locker room," Halvonik remembered.

"What I remember was that there was a sense of huge frustration," Feinstein said. "There wasn't any type of physical confrontation. If there had been, I would have written about it."

In postgame interviews, Pitt's players did question their direction in the closing moments of the game.

"The players made no attempt to hide their anger," Halvonik said. "Some of them were openly critical of Paul afterward."

"Had Feinstein not told the other writers what he'd witnessed, in my opinion, a lot of the negativity that surrounded that incident—that was reported and grew a life of its own—might not have happened," Eldridge said. "Paul got painted by a pretty heavy brush by the media for that."

El-Amin's Killer Move
Impressed Kid Krauser

Pitt's devastating 70-69 home loss to undefeated and No. 1-ranked Connecticut on December 12, 1998, had a positive spin, although nobody inside Fitzgerald Field House realized it at the time.

Pitt's quaint home facility was jammed that afternoon, with fans having been urged to wear white to the game. The Panthers led the entire game. But UConn's Khalid El-Amin stole an errant Pitt inbounds pass with a few seconds remaining, brought the ball to the hoop without much resistance, and killed the Panthers' upset hopes with a game-winning shot at the buzzer.

One person who wasn't at the game was impressed by the Pitt spectacle, nonetheless. Seventeen-year-old Carl Krauser had watched the game on television from his home in New York.

"Vonteego Cummings, Kellii Taylor, and Jarrett Lockhart were the Pitt players I remember," Krauser said. "In the last second, Khalid El-Amin hit a tough shot to beat them. He jumped up on the table after that. I just said, 'Ah, man, I need to be there.' I didn't know they allowed you to do that—jumping on tables—in college. I wanted to be in a crazy environment like that, where people love to play basketball."

The experience gave Krauser a strong sense of where he wanted to play his college ball.

"I just wanted to come to Pitt after that," he said. "I remembered how fired up the crowd was. I was impressed by that."

Barlow Learned His Lesson

Kevan Barlow's career almost didn't make it to his junior year. The multitalented running back from Pittsburgh's Peabody High School teased Pitt's coaches and fans with his outstanding strength and agility, but his work ethic and commitment to the program were sometimes questionable. After failing to show for a treatment session at the Pitt Stadium training room before 1999 spring practice, coach Walt Harris summoned Barlow to his office for a talk.

Barlow began spring practice on schedule but was eventually suspended by Harris, who wanted another meeting with the player.

"I had to do everything right," Barlow said. "I had to do everything they asked of me. No parking tickets, no nothing. I could not do anything wrong."

The message got through. Barlow, who scored the last touchdown at Pitt Stadium in the win against Notre Dame in 1999, capped his college career in Pittsburgh by running all over West Virginia in the last college game played at Three Rivers Stadium in 2000. Barlow's day included 277 yards and four touchdowns in Pitt's 38-28 victory.

"It was a blessing in disguise," he remarked, when asked about the suspension. "I think I needed it to wake me up."

CHAPTER THREE

RIVALS

0-0, 0-0, 0-0

Jock Sutherland's Pitt football teams of the 1930s dominated Eastern football, but they had their hands full with the Fordham Rams. Pitt and Fordham battled to scoreless ties in 1935 and 1936, but the Panthers were confident they would break the streak when they met Fordham at New York's Polo Grounds on October 16, 1937.

Pitt's great halfback, Marshall Goldberg, scored on a 14-yard run to give the Panthers an apparent lead, but there was a flag on the play.

"Tony Matisi was called for holding on the play," Goldberg said. "The funny thing was, the guy he was supposed to be blocking, I don't think he even moved on the play. Whatever Tony did had absolutely no bearing on the play. But what can you do? That was the call."

"If it is true, as the saying goes, that a tie is like kissing your sister, the men who in the mid-1930s played football for Fordham and Pittsburgh to this day hold the all-time American record for, well, simulated incest," Myron Cope wrote in the *Pitt Alumni Times*.

Goldberg did score the first touchdown the following year (1938), when the Panthers broke the scoreless streak with a 24-13 win against the Rams at a jam-packed Pitt Stadium.

Is There a Doctor on the Bench?

Pitt's Eddie Straloski, nicknamed "The Polish Flyer" by Pittsburgh sportswriters, was one of the more gregarious members of the Panthers' 1940-1941 basketball team, but smiling and laughing were the last things on his mind following the Panthers' 56-45 win against West Virginia at the Pitt Stadium Pavilion on Febuary 11, 1941.

The Panthers and Mountaineers, basketball rivals since 1906, met only one time during Pitt's "Final Four" season, but the spectators who made their way to the Pavilion that night were treated to more than a basketball game.

The fun started just five minutes into the game when Straloski, who later changed his name to Strall, was fouled hard by WVU's Rudy Baric while driving for a basket. Straloski hit the cement wall beyond the basket and lay motionless for better than a minute, according to a *Pittsburgh Press* account of the incident. Smelling salts, administered by coach Doc Carlson, were needed to revive him.

But the main event took place in the second half when Straloski, after jostling with Mountaineer Scotty Hamilton for a loose ball, tossed the ball upward, a seemingly innocent act. The ball, unfortunately, struck Hamilton, who did not see Straloski release it. Thinking it was a deliberate act, Hamilton floored Straloski with one quick punch to the jaw, bringing angry Pitt players and fans off the bench and out of the stands. Several Pitt players went after Hamilton, and police were required to restore order—or so it seemed.

Hamilton was ejected from the game, and while being led from the court, a photographer tried to snap a picture. The attempt angered some of Hamilton's teammates, who chased the man with the camera up into the stands.

The episode brought athletics officials from both schools to courtside, including West Virginia football coach Bill Kern, a former Pitt football star and later top assistant to Jock Sutherland. Pitt athletic director James Hagan and football coach Charley Bowser also acted as peacemakers.

After the game, Hamilton visited the Pitt locker room to apologize.

"This is the worst thing that ever happened to me," Hamilton told *The Pittsburgh Press*. "I don't know why I did it. I hope you can understand how sorry I am."

John Swacus, a member of that Pitt team, remembered the incident more than 60 years later.

"It was something that shouldn't have happened," Swacus explained. "It wasn't meant to happen. Hamilton thought Eddie threw the ball at him deliberately, but he didn't. It wasn't a vindictive thing. Eddie was walking away from the play when he tossed the ball up."

Carlson placed the blame for the affair at the feet of that night's officials—Harold Alison and Howard Campbell.

"They call a lot of petty fouls that get the boys so incensed and stirred up that they don't know what they're doing," he told reporters. "In the Midwest and East, officials at least give the boys a chance to play the game."

Straloski, who later served as basketball and baseball coach at Bethel (now Bethel Park) High School in suburban Pittsburgh, was not the type of person who went looking for trouble.

"He was a tremendous player and a fun person to be around," Swacus said. "He had a great sense of humor, and he was the type who liked to play jokes on people. Even now, I can see his face, like a little kid looking to get into some type of mischief."

The Doc and Chick Show

It is interesting to note that, in Doc Carlson's last 14 seasons as coach of the Panthers, Pitt and Duquesne never met on the basketball court. Not in a regular-season game, that is.

"We used to scrimmage Pitt a lot," said Red Manning, who was a Duquesne freshman in 1947-1948. "One time my freshman year—I wasn't eligible to play then—the varsity scrimmaged Pitt at our campus gym. [Charles] Chick Davies was our coach. He and Doc put on quite a show. And this was just a scrimmage! A Pitt player got hurt and was down. Doc went over to him and said, 'C'mon, get up! You have one good lung left.'"

A popular story about Carlson is how he liked to serve his players ice cream.

"It's true," Manning said. "When I was at Duquesne, we liked to scrimmage Pitt because Doc would give all the players ice cream at halftime. I think it was North Pole Ice Cream. I don't know if he had an interest in them."

Bill Baierl, who played at Pitt during the late 1940s, confirmed Manning's suspicion.

"People called us 'The Ice Cream Eaters,'" Baierl said. "The first day of practice, we'd have a publicity picture taken of all the players eating ice cream, but after that, no more ice cream. We'd be sucking oranges."

A Free Point for the Mountaineers

West Virginia's Mountaineers were riding high with a 7-0 record when they came to Pitt Stadium to play the Panthers on November 12, 1955. Officials from the Sugar Bowl also were on hand to scout the sixth-ranked Mountaineers as a possible team for the New Year's Day game. The men from New Orleans left the press box beaming over the Panthers.

Pitt defeated WVU with relative ease, 26-7, but one prominent Pitt man wasn't smiling at game's end. Assistant coach Steve Petro was fit to be tied.

"West Virginia scored on the last play, but by that time one of the goalposts was already down," Beano Cook remembered. "Steve Petro was pacing the sideline. The officials and both coaches agreed to just give West Virginia the extra point. Petro was raising hell about it. He didn't want to give the point to West Virginia."

It took a while for Petro to calm down, but he had to be happy when the Sugar Bowl ultimately selected Pitt—not West Virginia—for its game. Cook believes the win against West Virginia was a significant one in Panthers' history.

"That win put Pitt back into national prominence in college football," he said. "Despite all the stupid decisions made by the eggheads who sat in the Cathedral of Learning, starting in the late '30s, it took that many years to get back, but it wasn't very long before the eggheads were at it again."

Cooperative Rivals

Pitt's original 1958-1959 basketball schedule had the Panthers and Penn State slated to meet twice, with the February 28 season finale set for Rec Hall. Because that would be the last game for Pitt's Don Hennon, Pitt's athletic director asked his Penn State colleague to do Pitt a favor.

"Frank Carver called Ernie McCoy to see if we could switch the sites, because we wanted to have a special night for Don Hennon," Beano Cook recalled. "Penn State agreed to it. That would never happen today. The relations were good then."

The Panthers won the game, 84-65, and Hennon had his moment in the spotlight. Hennon later received a call from Bob Prince, who broadcast Pitt basketball games on the radio at the time.

"Prince said he had a gift for him," Cook said. "[Prince] gave Don a microscope that he could use when he went on to medical school."

Petro Says We Should Try This

It was getting late in the fourth quarter at Mountaineer Field on October 19, 1963. The undefeated Panthers trailed West Virginia 10-7 and were having a hard time solving the Mountaineers' defense. Pitt had the ball at the WVU 46-yard line. It was time for a suggestion.

"[Assistant coach] Steve Petro was sitting beside me in the coaches' booth up above," offensive coordinator Bimbo Cecconi recalled. "There was a certain play he wanted us to run. 'We're due for that play,' he said."

The play was 27 Reverse, and 46 yards later, the Panthers had the lead for good, even though the extra point failed.

"It was a reverse play that went in for a score," Cecconi said. "Steve had been hounding us to call it. I was calling the plays, and Steve requested it. It's a play we had used before, but maybe not in that game. The ball went to Bill Bodle, who gave it to Paul Martha, and Martha came back to the right and took it in."

The victory was especially significant for the Panthers, who were trying to continue their unbeaten season—and to impress the rest of the nation.

"John Underwood from *Sports Illustrated* was at that game to do a story about Pitt," said Beano Cook, then the Panthers' sports information director. "I remember overhearing him on the phone at halftime, talking to someone back at his office, saying how Pitt might lose this game."

Pitt-West Virginia has always been a special game to Cecconi, who played for the Panthers and later served as an assistant under two different head coaches.

"All the times we played them were memorable," he said. "Once in a while they'll whip us, or we'll whip them, but, for the most part, they've always been exciting games."

The Basket Didn't Count

By his estimation, Dave Roman still hears about it at least once a week.

"It" happened on a Saturday night, February 2, 1963, when the West Virginia Mountaineers visited Pitt at the Field House. WVU led 68-67, and there were three seconds left on the old scoreboard clock. The Panthers, huddled with coach Bob Timmons, would put the ball in play at half court.

"In the huddle, Coach Timmons gave us two options, and we did both," Roman said. "I was having a pretty good game. One play was set up to get the ball to me, and if I could get open for a shot, I was to take the shot. If we couldn't do that, we were just to get the ball in play and call time right away."

The game, telecast locally, had the big Field House crowd howling.

"I broke free, right over the 10-second line," Roman said. "I got the ball and put it up. I knew it was good. The hoop looked like a big bushel basket when I shot it."

Fans stormed the court. Students and players hoisted Roman on their shoulders. There was only one problem: The game wasn't over.

"Things got quiet," Roman said. "We saw the referees and the coaches over at the scorer's table talking about it. I looked up at the scoreboard. There was still one second left, and we were still down by one."

"It was the right call," said Beano Cook, Pitt's sports information director who served as color analyst on the telecast of the game.

As the play developed, Pitt's Ben Jinks—away from the ball—had called for time.

"The timer that night was Bobby Lewis, the Pitt baseball coach at the time," Roman said. "I think if Bobby had just let the clock expire, we would have had the win. But he recognized that time had been called, and he stopped the clock."

The Panthers still had one second for another shot, but it misfired.

"I got letters from people for several weeks after that, from people sympathizing with me for what had happened," Roman said. "[*Pitt News* writer] Jim O'Brien did a big interview with me after that."

Eleven nights later in Morgantown, the Panthers faced the Mountaineers in a rematch. That game featured the ejections of Brian Generalovich and West Virginia's Gale Catlett for fighting. Generalovich remembers it well.

"Gale was very scrappy, a strong player," he said. "He always seemed to draw me whenever we'd go man-to-man. We would go at it underneath."

The Panthers had their revenge. Final score: Pitt 69, WVU 68.

December 7, 1963

This was no Day of Infamy for die-hard Pitt fans, particularly for the school's eccentric sports information director.

"It was one of the best days of my life," Beano Cook said. "To win a football game [against Penn State] by one point and the basketball game against another big rival [Duquesne]—that was a big day."

For the record, Pitt beat Penn State 22-21 on a fourth-quarter run by quarterback Fred Mazurek. That game was played two weeks later than its originally scheduled date—November 23—because of the assassination of President John F. Kennedy. Later that evening, the Pitt basketball Panthers downed Duquesne 69-67 in overtime in the finals of the Steel Bowl Tournament at the Pitt Field House.

The basketball game featured a highly publicized brush-off between a pair of old friends and teammates, and a very strange ending.

Generalovich and Somerset had grown up and played ball together, and were teammates at Farrell High School, but that familiarity went out the window when their college teams met in basketball.

"That was a typical Pitt-Duquesne game—very, very rough," Generalovich said. "Cegalis and I had been getting tangled up inside the whole game. Willie and I had gotten tangled up a few times, but that was just in the course of the game. We certainly weren't going after each other."

A Generalovich roadblock, however, changed things.

"Somebody had the ball for us, and Willie switched on him," Generalovich said. "Willie didn't see where I was. I was setting a pick high to get one of our guys free, and Willie ran right into me. He was about 180 pounds. I was 220. He got knocked to the floor."

As an act of sportsmanship, Generalovich reached down to help Somerset.

"He slapped my hand away," Generalovich recalled. "After the game we hugged and apologized, but I remember the media making a big deal out of what happened. But that was a great game from a fan's standpoint."

"Willie was such a nice kid," Duquesne coach Red Manning said. "I'm sure it was just one of those things done in frustration. That was a tough way to lose."

With Pitt holding a 69-67 lead and the clock winding down in overtime, Duquesne's John Cegalis made an apparent game-tying shot to send the contest into a second extra session. But, after the officials conferred with timekeeper Leo "Horse" Czarnecki, the basket was ruled no good.

"In my mind, time had run out," said Manning. "I remember looking at the clock as time wound down. I think we still had one timeout left. I knew it was going to be a close call."

What makes the story so unusual is that the game officials deferred to Czarnecki's judgment

"He was the timer," Cook said. "Needless to say, Duquesne complained. To this day, Duquesne thinks it got robbed. But 'Horse' [a Pitt employee and groundskeeper] was honest. Still, I can understand why Duquesne fans would be upset."

"It was just one of those things," Manning said. "But that was a pretty tough task, putting 'Horse' on the clock like that."

36-35

Pitt was on the verge of completing a remarkable comeback on October 17, 1970, at Pitt Stadium. After trailing West Virginia 35-8 at halftime, the Panthers pulled to within 35-30 with 55 seconds remaining. It was third down, four yards to go, at the WVU five-yard line.

The Panthers had been churning up ground throughout the second half, and had rallied without the benefit of big plays from their offense. So, what play would be called for quarterback Dave Havern?

"I really didn't know what to expect," Havern said. "Finally, when the play came in, I'll never forget, it was 58X Delay, a pass. I thought, 'Who the hell called this play?'"

It turned out to be offensive coordinator Bimbo Cecconi, although Havern wouldn't discover that until much later.

"I had to see who 'X' was in that formation," Havern recalled. "I thought it was probably Steve Moyer, our best receiver. But it was Bill Pilconis. We ran the play, and he was so wide open I couldn't believe it."

There was more excitement after the game, just outside the West Virginia locker room inside Gate 3 at Pitt Stadium. Angry Mountaineer fans, upset with the conservative second-half play selection of first-year coach Bobby Bowden, pounded on the Mountaineers' clubhouse door.

"I think if I had gone out there, they would have lynched me right on the spot," said Bowden, many years later.

Role Reversal for Pitt and Duquesne

Everybody loves a winner, and for those Pittsburghers who followed college basketball from the 1940s to 1970s, that usually meant the Duquesne Dukes, not the Pitt Panthers. People whose names are associated with Pitt once called Duquesne their team.

"I loved Duquesne basketball [in the 1940s]," Beano Cook said. "I can remember going in Christmastime in 1946 to a doubleheader at the old Duquesne Gardens with Westminster playing Harvard and Duquesne playing Holy Cross. I really didn't get interested in Pitt until I went to school there."

Bill Hillgrove, a Duquesne graduate who became the basketball voice of the Panthers in 1969, tells a similar tale:

"Duquesne had the great teams back then," Hillgrove said. "Teams with Dick Ricketts, Jim Tucker, and Sihugo Green. Duquesne in the '50s had not only good players, but great players. A lot of conferences would not allow black players, so several of the Catholic schools opened their doors to the black athlete. Duquesne was the first team, excluding predominantly black colleges, with the opportunity to start five black players."

Pitt and Duquesne first met on the court in 1932 and met regularly at the Pitt Stadium Pavilion. Both schools also sponsored boxing as an intercollegiate sport and scheduled a few boxing-basketball doubleheaders for Pittsburgh fans. Unfortunately, the fisticuffs often continued on the basketball court, and the schools ceased playing each other from 1940 to 1952.

An in-season tournament called the Steel Bowl revived the series in 1953, and construction of the Pitt Field House brought the Dukes to the Oakland campus throughout that decade. In fact, Duquesne used Pitt's facility as its home court for several years. Point Park College also played its home games at the Field House for a while.

On December 6, 1961, Pitt and Duquesne christened the brand new Civic Arena in downtown Pittsburgh with a college basketball doubleheader. Pitt played Ohio State (featuring Jerry Lucas, John Havlicek, and Bobby Knight) while the Dukes hosted Carnegie Tech. Still, Pitt and Duquesne would not schedule any regular-season contests—only a chance meeting in the Steel Bowl, eventually played at the arena.

The Steel Bowl games were special games for the participants and their respective followers. In previewing the 1973 game at the Civic Arena, Jeff Samuels wrote for *The Press*:

"[The rivalry] makes the city vibrate. It's one of the few times a year that mention of the word basketball won't provoke a massive yawn."

The formation of the Eastern Eight in 1976 meant at least two games each season for the rivals, and the games played from 1976-1982 were among the most fiercely contested games in the country. Many of the players were local, a factor that added to the drama and interest. Fights were commonplace—on the court and in the stands.

"Usually in a rivalry, there's a certain level of mutual respect, but not with that one," said Mike Rice, a Duquesne graduate who coached the Dukes from 1978 to 1982. "I broadcast games for ESPN, and I've seen a lot of great rivalries in basketball, at both the high school and college levels, but there was a special kind of hate involved with Pitt-Duquesne."

"I have a hard time explaining to people just how great our rivalry with Duquesne was," said Tim Grgurich, who coached the Panthers from 1975 to 1980. "We had some real battles with them to get the good kids from western Pennsylvania to come to Pitt. I hated losing a kid to Duquesne. People don't realize what it was like for us to beat Duquesne, or Duquesne to beat West Virginia, or West Virginia to beat us. It was like our own little world."

Grgurich's chief recruiting rival at Duquesne was John Cinicola, an assistant to Red Manning who became the Dukes' head coach in 1974. He remembers the personal animosity generated by the rivalry.

"Tim and I never spoke," Cinicola said. "It wasn't until the [Eastern Eight] conference was formed, when we were both head coaches, that we finally had to open up to each other."

One funny episode occurred at Fitzgerald Field House on February 22, 1978. The Panthers were on their way to a 72-65 win against the Dukes, and Cinicola took exception to Pitt's pep band playing at what he believed were inappropriate times. He went to complain to the officials, gesturing toward the band. Grgurich, taking the cue, motioned for the band to keep right on playing.

"That's the way it was in those games," Cinicola said. "And then all the fights we had. They all kind of run together when you try to remember one."

Roy Chipman, who replaced Grgurich as Pitt's coach in 1980, was caught off guard by the intensity of the rivalry.

"I had heard a lot about it when I came to Pittsburgh, but it was even more than I expected," Chipman said. "Even when we went to the Big East, none of those games with Syracuse or Georgetown were as intense as the games with Duquesne. The first hard foul, it seemed everybody was ready to fight."

Chipman, who died in 1997, recognized the "good old days" for the Pitt-Duquesne rivalry were most likely coming to an end when Pitt accepted an invitation to join a new conference in 1982.

"What happened when we went to the Big East was that we were then competing at a different level," he explained. "As a result, the Duquesne game was no longer as important to Pitt."

Good Measuring Sticks for Majors's First Pitt Team

Notre Dame and Penn State both finished with perfect 12-0-0 records in 1973, and Johnny Majors's first Pitt team was able to judge how far it had progressed while playing both teams. The Panthers lost to the Fighting Irish 31-10 at Pitt Stadium, and the Nittany Lions rallied to win 35-13 in the regular-season finale at Beaver Stadium.

"What I remember the most about Notre Dame is how physically dominating they were," said Billy Daniels, Pitt's quarterback that season. "Penn State might have been a shade behind as far as size and speed, but I had the sense [Penn State] was better coached. Back then, Notre Dame relied on its superiority from a talent standpoint."

Freshman Tony Dorsett ran for 209 yards against the Irish, but Pitt shot itself in the foot with crucial turnovers throughout the game. The new-look Panthers then found themselves in a classic

*Freshman Tony Dorsett ran for 209 yards against
Notre Dame in a 1973 game at Pitt Stadium.*
Photo courtesy of the University of Pittsburgh Athletic Department

smashmouth game against the Lions, long before the term became familiar to football fans.

"In the huddle, we had one offensive lineman who was crying because [Penn State defensive lineman] Mike Hartenstine was just beating the hell out of him on every play," Daniels said. "Another one of our guys had his lower tooth coming through his lower lip and was bleeding profusely."

Pitt took a 13-3 halftime lead on a 50-yard field goal by Carson Long at the end of the second quarter, but Penn State—with Heisman Trophy winner John Cappelletti—was too strong in the second half.

"Penn State kicked off to us to start the second half, and we were stuck deep in our territory," Daniels recalled. "We were surrounded by their student section, and they were going berserk. We could hardly hear in the huddle. I was screaming at the top of my lungs just to get the play called. We had been doing reasonably well up until that point, but they just took control of the game. It showed how much a crowd could inspire a team."

Get That Nittany Lion Off My Back!

Only one team, Penn State, stood between the 1976 Pitt football team, the Sugar Bowl with Georgia, and a perfect season. Pitt had lost 10 straight to the Nittany Lions, none as crushing as the 7-6 defeat at Three Rivers Stadium the year before.

"That was really the first time that we outplayed them," said John Majors, Pitt's coach. "I don't believe in saying 'should have' and 'could have,' but we outplayed them that day."

The nightmarish loss included three missed field goals by Carson Long, along with a blocked extra point. Pitt's spectacular wide receiver, the elusive Gordon Jones, took a pass from Matt Cavanaugh at the Penn State 10-yard line late in the game but turned toward the sideline rather than inside (and a sure touchdown). The Penn State defensive back who had been covering Jones slipped, enabling him to trip the receiver from a prone position, maybe a first.

In any event, the 1976 game was crucial to Pitt's program for a number of reasons. The first half ended with the score 7-7. It was a time for an adjustment.

"We came out the second half and started with [Tony] Dorsett at fullback," Majors recalled. "The first time we moved him, ever, to fullback, he went about 40 yards for a touchdown. [Penn State] misadjusted in the middle. We hit the middle just right, and there was nobody in the middle. He ran right past the goalpost."

Pitt had enjoyed a week off before the Penn State game and put in a few wrinkles, one out of necessity.

"We put in the I formation after [Matt] Cavanaugh was injured [against Louisville in the fifth game]," Majors said. "I told the staff I was gonna put in the unbalanced line. That would change the blocking schemes, but we put in a couple simple plays, with Dorsett at fullback."

The 24-7 victory against Pitt's archrival left Majors so excited, he never went to bed that night.

Who Has the Flu?

One of the most spirited basketball rivalries during Pitt's pre-Big East years was the Villanova series that began in the late 1970s.

Following a disastrous 6-21 season in 1976-1977, the Panthers bounced back the following year and were set to meet the Wildcats in a key league matchup in mid-February 1978. A sickly thing, however, happened to Villanova on the way to Fitzgerald Field House, although Pitt fans weren't buying any of it.

"I remember it like it was yesterday," said current Wildcats broadcaster Whitey Rigsby, a starting guard for Villanova that season. "We were supposed to go out to Pittsburgh for the game, and 90 percent of our team caught the Russian Flu. My girlfriend at the time—now my wife—lived a block down from the campus, and she caught it, too. Her mother was taking care of both of us."

The game was not played as scheduled, and Pitt fans smelled a rat, suspecting that Villanova backed out of the game to buy time for injured star forward Alex Bradley.

"It was legitimate," Rigsby maintains. "There's no way we would have had enough players to suit up."

When Villanova took the court in Pittsburgh for the rescheduled game on February 18, 1978, Pitt students let them have it with a steady chorus of "Who's Got the Flu? ...Who's Got The Flu?"

"We ended up getting killed anyway," Rigsby said.

Pitt won 97-81, despite 35 points from Bradley.

"Those were good games against Pitt," Rigsby said. "I remember Sam Clancy and Wayne Williams. Larry Harris was a great shooter.

"That rivalry didn't exist before then and didn't really start up again until later in the Big East years. I did a game here on television where [coaches] Rollie Massimino and Paul Evans had to be separated coming off the court."

A Backyard Mismatch

The Pitt-West Virginia football rivalry has come to be known as The Backyard Brawl. Although nobody can say for sure how or when that label originated, the games were anything but competitive during Jackie Sherrill's years (1977-1981) in Pittsburgh. His teams swept five games from WVU.

The Panthers received a full dose of the West Virginians' venom the night before the final college football game was played at old Mountaineer Field in November 1979. WVU fans were out en masse outside the Holiday Inn in Morgantown, next door to the Coliseum.

"Their fans just hated us with a passion," Pitt offensive tackle Mark May said. "The night before that game, out in the parking lot at the hotel, people were making noise until four in the morning. They were partying, yelling... anything they could do to try to disturb us."

The fans were no less enthusiastic the next day at the game.

"In the locker room before the game, Coach Sherrill told the younger players not to take their helmets off on the sideline," May said. "They were throwing everything at us."

Pitt won that game, 24-17, the closest Backyard Brawl during Sherrill's term, and quarterback Dan Marino's second career start as a true freshman.

In Sherrill's five games against WVU, Pitt outscored the Mountaineers 179-41.

Williamson's Interception

Darkness was approaching, light snow was falling, and Penn State's offense was driving for what could have been a game-winning touchdown. Pitt strong safety Carlton Williamson, however, put an end to the Nittany Lions' upset hopes by making an interception at the Pitt 31-yard line with only 46 seconds remaining.

Both Pitt and Penn State sported 9-1 records going into their November 28, 1980, meeting at Beaver Stadium. The Panthers were ranked fourth, Penn State fifth. A loss would have been especially devastating for the Panthers, who entered the season with a legitimate shot to claim a national title.

Pitt was ahead 14-9 after three quarters, and its top-rated defense was put to a supreme test in the final period. Penn State entered Pitt territory three times and came away with zero points. Just moments before Williamson's interception, Penn State had a fourth-and-one situation at the Pitt 37. A blitzing Sal Sunseri forced quarterback Todd Blackledge to make his pitch to Curt Warner prematurely. Rickey Jackson, Williamson, and cornerback Lynn Thomas surrounded Warner and dropped him for a three-yard loss.

On the final drive, Blackledge had scrambled for a first down at the Pitt 34 on another fourth-down play. The Nittany Lions, going without a huddle, hurried to the line of scrimmage. Blackledge took a quick drop, and threw toward the Pitt sideline, where Williamson made his big play.

"I think [Blackledge] was trying to make the completion," Williamson told reporters in the happy Pitt locker room. "He didn't see me break out there; he never saw me."

"It was a sprint out, and I was actually trying to throw it out of bounds and stop the clock," Blackledge said. "I never saw the guy."

48-14

The score, a freak of nature, produces a flood of painful memories for Pitt players, coaches, and fans.

"That's a game I have not ever watched again," said John Brown, a junior tight end that season.

"I literally saw some of our players crying after the game," remarked Alex Kramer, the team's administrative assistant.

"That game was an aberration," said Foge Fazio, Pitt's defensive coordinator. "That was a lowlight for us, especially at the end of the year, and because of what was at stake."

Pitt was 10-0 and ranked No. 1 in the nation. Penn State was 8-2 when it visited a sold-out Pitt Stadium on November 28, 1981, Pitt coach Jackie Sherrill's 38th birthday. Portable bleachers were installed in the end zone to accommodate the overflow crowd on a cold, gray, blustery day. The Panthers had already secured a Sugar Bowl date with Georgia. Beat Penn State, and Pitt was one win away from a national championship.

Dan Marino threw touchdown passes to Dwight Collins on Pitt's first two possessions. The Nittany Lions were held without a first down in the first quarter. Leading 14-0 and with the ball at the Penn State 31-yard line to start the second quarter, Marino threw a pass toward Julius Dawkins at the back of the end zone.

"[Dawkins] just got blown up on the play," was how Fazio described the jarring hit that resulted in an interception by Roger Jackson.

Penn State took the ball the length of the field for a score and then tied the game on a touchdown run by Todd Blackledge. It was 14-14 at halftime.

Pitt turned the ball over early in the third quarter, and Blackledge hit Kenny Jackson for a pair of long touchdown passes. The Panthers trailed 28-14.

"On offense and defense, we started trying to do things just to win the game right then," Fazio said. "We panicked. In the secondary, we had some guys going the wrong way, playing the wrong coverages."

The ultimate hurt came late in the game, when Penn State's Mark Robinson intercepted a Marino pass and worked his way through the Panthers' offense for a 91-yard interception return for a touchdown.

"I knew then that we didn't have a chance," Fazio said.

Ironically, Penn State was ranked higher than Pitt going into the 1981 season. The Panthers had defeated the Nittany Lions—both times at Beaver Stadium—in 1979 and 1980 but had sustained huge personnel losses from the 1980 club. Penn State actually spent a week at No. 1 in the polls in 1981, until losing at Miami in October. Alabama also defeated Penn State that year.

"Penn State had a pretty good team that year," Fazio said. "They had a lot better team than some people thought they were."

"Their receivers that year were probably the best that they had ever had at Penn State," Sherrill added.

"What made that game approach the freak-of-nature level wasn't so much that we lost," Brown said. "It was the final score."

Hamilton and Gilbert

West Virginia football coach Don Nehlen was previewing the 1991 Pitt-WVU game in Morgantown, the first ever Big East Football Conference game for both schools. A Pittsburgh writer wanted to know Nehlen's opinion of Pitt's mammoth defensive ends, six-foot-seven, 270-pound Keith Hamilton and six-foot-six, 300-pound Sean Gilbert.

"If those are the first two guys we see getting off the bus, we might just turn around and go home," Nehlen explained.

Nehlen had cause for concern. The Panthers, a slight underdog entering the game, manhandled the Mountaineers on a beautiful Saturday night ESPN telecast from Morgantown. Pitt won 34-3, and Gilbert shook the Mountaineer Field turf with a 26-yard interception return for a touchdown in the third quarter.

Fourth and 17

Pitt trailed West Virginia 38-35 in the third overtime period on November 28, 1997, at Mountaineer Field. Needing a victory to become bowl-eligible, the Panthers faced a fourth-and-17 play.

"[West Virginia] was in a coverage that should have been a single safety robbing the crossing area, along with the deep safety," Pitt coach Walt Harris remembered. "What happened was, they busted; both guys went deep. There was nobody right there. Jake Hoffart beat his man, and Pete [Gonzalez] made the throw."

Following an incomplete pass to Chris Schneider, Gonzalez found Terry Murphy in the end zone for the touchdown pass to give Pitt a 41-38 win—and its first bowl bid since 1989. Harris recalled the aftermath of the play, as Pitt people went wild, and West Virginia supporters were stunned.

"It was unbelievably wild," Harris said. "I don't think I've ever been involved in one quite as wild as that."

Almost

Few observers gave Pitt's football team much of a chance against Penn State when the Panthers visited Beaver Stadium on September 11, 1999. Pitt was coming off a 2-9 season, while the Nittany Lions were serious national title contenders.

After a late field goal gave Penn State a 20-17 lead, Pitt's Hank Poteat came close to breaking the ensuing kickoff return for a go-ahead touchdown. Still, the Panthers had the ball in Penn State territory.

"[Penn State] was probably lucky to get out of the game with a three-point victory," Pitt coach Walt Harris said. "On our final drive, we had a sack right before the last field goal attempt. We had a good play called, but one of our best receivers just kind of blanked and kept running, and the quarterback [John Turman] kept waiting and took a sack."

Nick Lotz's 50-yard field goal attempt—Pitt's last gasp—was blocked by LaVar Arrington.

"The sack made our kicker have to kick a longer kick," Harris said. "He kicked it flatter. LaVar Arrington made a play that super men make, and he was a great player. But our guys played hard and over their heads against a team that was very talented."

Retaliation

It was the biggest, most anticipated home game in the history of the University of Pittsburgh's basketball program. Pitt and Connecticut, teams which had played for the Big East Tournament title the previous two seasons, met before a jam-packed sellout crowd of 12,817 at the Petersen Events Center on February 15, 2004.

Pitt "held serve," was how UConn coach Jim Calhoun described Pitt's 75-68 win, a game in which the Panthers never trailed. Rivalries are at their best when two teams are fighting for the same prize, and that's what was at stake when Pitt and Connecticut met during this period.

The Huskies defeated the Panthers at the Hartford Civic Center earlier in the season, so the Panthers were looking for revenge—as well as first place in the Big East standings. UConn was an overwhelming preseason pick for No. 1 in the Big East, and at least one Panther was tired of hearing it.

"I keep hearing about how much more talented UConn is supposed to be than us, but I don't see it," said Julius Page, who scored 11 points in the rematch.

Calhoun, who that day was notified that he was a candidate for induction into the Basketball Hall of Fame, gave the Panthers their due.

"They have a lot of kids on their team with bravado," he said. "They play very physical defense. That may be the best job anybody has done on Emeka [Okafor, the Huskies' star center]."

Julius Page dunks it home.
Photo courtesy of the University of Pittsburgh Athletic Department

Special T-shirts bearing the inscription "Retaliation" sold out well before the game. The atmosphere was appreciated by Calhoun, who was much less enamored with Pitt's former facility, Fitzgerald Field House.

"It's a real good environment to play in here," he said. "This is a wonderful place to play."

Like a great heavyweight boxing match, the Pitt-UConn games represent the classic "Slugger against Speed" format, the Panthers slugging and the Huskies running.

"When [Pitt] gets ahead, they're a son of a gun, because they're gonna run their system every time down the court," Calhoun said.

Pitt-UConn Heats Up

When it comes to being first in the Big East, Connecticut and Pitt play for keeps.

The heated rivalry all began in 2002 when UConn claimed the Big East title in overtime with a 74-65 win. The next year the Panthers took conference honors with a 74-56 victory, and in 2004 the Panthers were trying to keep the glory at Pitt for the second straight year.

"Last year, we kicked their ass," former coach Ben Howland said, putting heavy emphasis on those last three words. "I don't think there was any question who was the best team a year ago in that tournament. I still think Pitt was the best team this year."

Strong words, but the competitive bickering doesn't start there. In 2003 after a 71-67 Huskies loss to the Panthers at the Petersen Events Center UConn coach Jim Calhoun was asked to assess Pitt.

"I don't think they're the most talented team in the Big East, but I think they're the best team in the Big East," was his reply.

The remark was open to a number of interpretations. Howland didn't appreciate it.

"I took exception to that," Howland said, "just to protect my players, which was the right thing to do."

Then came the 2003 Big East title game, but that didn't cool things down. The rivalry continued in 2004 with each team winning one regular-season game. So Howland wasn't impressed by Connecticut's 61-58 come-from-behind victory against Pitt in the finals of the 2004 Big East Tournament.

"[UConn] was really lucky to win," said Howland, who left little doubt about his feelings for the team he left. "That was a tough loss for us. I watched that game, and we felt terrible for the players. I felt, though, it would be a good thing in terms of the NCAA Tournament, that it would be like Syracuse losing in the semis of the Big East [in 2002-2003], then winning it all. I had visions of that for this [2003-2004] Pitt team."

Knight and Krauser:
A Point Guard's Perspective

Just when Chris Thomas, Notre Dame's outstanding point guard, had seen the last of Brandin Knight in Big East competition, along came Carl Krauser.

"They both made their teams go," said Thomas in a 2004 interview. "They always give their teams a chance to win, and they both have the ability to step up and make big plays."

Thomas went head to head with both and developed a special respect for the new Panther—Krauser—on the block.

"Brandin Knight had quite a reputation, deservedly," Thomas said. "I really believe that Brandin's success fueled Carl to do what he has. I respect Krauser's game, because he had to come out from Brandin's shadow, and he's played very well."

The Big East battles, though intense on the court, never carried over when the games were over.

"Nobody hates anybody," Thomas said. "We all respect each other in the conference. Brandin and I stayed in touch. We talked before and after games."

Krauser, according to Thomas, talked more *during* games.

Notre Dame's Chris Thomas tries to defend Brandin Knight. After this
2002 loss to the Irish, Pitt won 40 consecutive home games.
Photo courtesy of the University of Pittsburgh Athletic Department

"Brandin was more of a 'I'll get into you, defensively' type," Thomas said. "Carl is an older, flashy kind of guy who really knows how to play. He's more of a [New York City summer league] Rucker-type trash talker, but that's good. I liked playing against both guys."

Krauser and Knight certainly weren't rivals as teammates.

"We both helped each other at the same time," Krauser said. "We both got after it. We're a couple of passionate players, a couple of passionate point guards going at it. He's from Jersey; I'm from New York."

"One of the keys to us really becoming a dominant team in my third year there was the fact that Brandin had an unbelievable level of competition every day in practice with Carl," Ben Howland said. "Carl was in his redshirt year. He pushed Brandin. Carl is an unbelievable competitor, and I think he really helped Brandin improve. They went at it. It was physical; it was intense. It raised Brandin's level with everybody else. As Brandin went, that's how we went. If he was playing and practicing as hard as he could, that was infectious on everybody else. Jaron [Brown] was like that, too. It helped Julius Page. It helped everybody."

CHAPTER FOUR

RECRUITING

You're Going to Pitt, Marshall

Marshall Goldberg is one of the legendary figures from Pitt's glorious decade of the 1930s, but if it hadn't been for a visit from Jock Sutherland to Elkins, West Virginia, Goldberg might have wound up drawing comparisons to the Four Horsemen, rather than contributing to Pitt's Dream Backfield of 1938.

"I was all set to go to South Bend," Goldberg said. "Then, all of a sudden, out of the clear blue sky, this meeting took place with the Pitt A.D. Whitey Hagan, Jock Sutherland, and my father, in my father's office. They called me up after they had talked, and everything was changed just like that. I was going to Pitt. My brother drove me to Pittsburgh, and then we took a bus to Johnstown for camp, and that was all there was to it. Back then, you didn't question what your parents told you."

Goldberg, who received recruiting inquiries from West Point, Marshall, West Virginia, Navy, and Notre Dame, remained Pitt's all-time leading rusher until Tony Dorsett topped his career mark as a sophomore in 1974. Goldberg rushed for 1,957 yards from 1936-1938. He also holds the unique distinction of having finished in the top three of the Heisman Trophy voting in two different years. Goldberg placed third in 1937 (Clint Frank of Yale was the winner) and second (to Texas Christian University's Davey O'Brien) in 1938, but admits he wasn't surprised by the results.

"The New York Athletic Club was in charge of the Heisman, and it was a restricted club," said Goldberg, a Jew. "I had little chance."

Doc Carlson: "Show Me the Players!"

Rather than search for basketball talent, Doc Carlson would invite players to the Pitt campus for an all-purpose recruiting visit.

"Back then you could bring players to campus and try them out," explained Bob Timmons, who replaced Carlson as Pitt's coach in 1953. "Doc would bring in five players every Saturday afternoon, and they would scrimmage down at the old Pitt Stadium gym [Pavilion]. He'd keep the best two or three. The next Saturday, he'd do the same thing. Pretty soon you'd have your recruiting class. You had to do it that way, because not much money was spent on basketball."

Timmons discovered that when he became Pitt's coach. The situation was magnified when the NCAA outlawed the "bring 'em in, try 'em out" method of recruiting.

"I had to fight to get money for scholarships and recruiting," Timmons said. "When the NCAA put that rule in, you had to go out and look for players. I had to recruit kids locally. [Pitt's administration] didn't want to spend any money on basketball."

The Coach's Kid from Wampum

Don Hennon was a shooting star for the basketball teams at Wampum (Pennsylvania) High School in the 1950s, where his father, L. Butler Hennon, was head coach. The elder Hennon was

Don Hennon was a first-team All-American in 1957-1958.
Photo courtesy of the University of Pittsburgh Athletic Department

noted for his innovative practice routines, and college coaches were well aware of his son's ability.

"We knew all the people at a lot of the colleges because of my dad," Don Hennon said. "He also knew Doc Carlson because my dad had taken some graduate courses at Pitt."

When the time came to choose a college, Hennon had plenty of options.

"I had about 80 offers," he said. "I visited a lot of schools, including Colgate, NC State, Duke, Maryland, Westminster, and Geneva. I think I went down to Duke three years in a row. I almost went there."

Pitt coach Bob Timmons was confident that young Hennon would come to Pittsburgh.

"We were pretty confident because Don was a very good student, and he wanted to study medicine," said Timmons, who died in April 2004. "Doc Carlson had talked to him about medicine and basketball. Don had a pretty good mind of his own. He wasn't too influenced by other people."

When the process was over, Timmons had his man.

"I finally decided to stay in this area because of the medical school," Hennon said, "and also because it was closer for my family to come see my games."

How Much Do You Weigh, Havern?

McKees Rock, Pennsylvania, produced college football quarterbacks at a dizzying rate during the mid- to late 1960s and early 1970s, including Pitt's Bob Medwid, Penn State's Chuck Burkhart and John Hufnagel, and Notre Dame's Tom Clements. But the most unlikely looking college quarterback-to-be, Dave Havern, made a significant contribution of his own to Pitt's program during that same era.

Havern only played one season at quarterback at Montour High School, where the Spartans were perennial winners. Montour, however, failed to make the WPIAL playoffs his final year, and

Havern turned his thoughts toward a possible football scholarship. He received feelers from, among others, Pitt and William & Mary. If first impressions meant anything, Havern didn't dazzle any of the recruiters.

"The guy from William & Mary said, 'How much do you weigh?'" Havern said. "I told him I was about 145. Actually, I was five foot eight, 135."

In his heart, there was only one place for Havern.

"I always had positive feelings about the University of Pittsburgh," he said. "I remembered the first game I saw at Pitt Stadium. I used to watch *The Doc Carlson Show* on TV."

Still, there was the size issue, but Havern found the perfect solution: He took to wearing a bulky sweater when a recruiter—particularly Pitt head coach Dave Hart—was scheduled to make a house call.

"I had a knit sweater that was soft, dirty brown," Havern said. "It made me look a little bigger than I really was. Even when I played in high school, I used to wear something underneath my jersey to give me a little boost."

There was an instant connection between Havern, the feisty high school senior, and Hart, the energetic young coach.

"Coach Hart could sell you the Brooklyn Bridge," said Havern. "He was a tremendous recruiter."

Havern and another McKees Rocks prospect, fullback Tony Esposito, made their visits to Pitt together and attended the annual Varsity Letter Club Dinner the night before at the Webster Hall Hotel.

"I was very impressed by the quality of people," Havern said. "A lot of the alums were there and I got to know some of them. Regis Toomey, the old actor, was there. I was sold."

Havern was feeling good about himself before the start of his freshman year but received a dose of reality when he made the move to Oakland that September.

"I remember getting out of the car in front of the dorms, and the first person I saw was [lineman] Howard Broadhead," Havern said. "He was about six foot four, 250—the biggest guy I ever saw, and he was wearing a lumberjack's shirt. That's when it hit me how small I really was."

It didn't take long for Havern to feel comfortable in his new environment.

"I fell in love with the campus," he said. "There was always something going on. You step out of the dorms, go one way and you had Gus Miller's [Newsstand] and The Original [Hot Dog]. You go the other way and you have the Cathedral of Learning, Heinz Chapel, and the Carnegie Museum. It was the kind of stuff that grade school field trips were made of when you were a kid."

Big Lucius

Jerome Lane, you have company.

Sixteen years before Lane sent Fitzgerald Field House into a frenzy by shattering a backboard in a televised game against Providence, a prospective Pitt Panther wreaked his own brand of havoc with the school's basketball facilities.

Pitt's players were anxious to meet six-foot-10, 220-pound Lucius Keese, a junior college player from Largo, Florida, whose basketball resume in JC included a 51-rebound game.

"It was around the time of the [Dapper Dan] Roundball when he came up for his official visit," said Kirk Bruce, then a team member. "[Assistant] coach [Tim] Grgurich was telling us about this big center who was coming up, so a bunch of us went to somebody's apartment in Oakland because that was where Coach Grgurich was gonna bring Lucius after he picked him up at the airport."

What happened next was similar to the *Munsters* television episode in which Leo Durocher, playing himself, invited Herman for a baseball tryout at a neighborhood field.

"We decided to take him up to the Field House and play for a while," Bruce said. "I don't know who it was, but somebody said, 'Hey, Lucius, let's see you dunk.' Well, this was on the main court. Lucius went up and dunked and actually bent the rim. This was before they had collapsible rims. So we said, 'Hey man, we better play at one of these side baskets.' They used to have sandbags at the base of these portable hoops to keep them in place. Well, Lucius dunks again, dislodges the bags and brings the whole basket down, rim first!"

The scrimmage over, Keese, who wore a size 17 shoe, eventually signed with the Panthers and earned his varsity 'P'—and the coveted letter jacket.

"When the weather was nice, a lot of students used to hang out at that patio just outside the Towers dorms," Bruce said. "You'd see your friends coming by after class or from leaving the cafeteria. The day Lucius got his letter jacket, a few of us were hanging around with him there, and he had his jacket off, draped over a railing. We made up a story to get him to walk away for a minute, something like, 'Hey, Lucius, that girl over there wants to talk to you.' So he left, and when he came back, his jacket was gone. And he was mad, almost to the point of being out of control. He was grabbing guys, and when he got hold of you, look out. He didn't realize his own strength."

Keese went after one of the biggest players in college basketball during his first season as a Panther. When Pitt played at UCLA on December 22, 1972, he was ejected from the game late in the second half after shoving Sven Nater, the Bruins' backup center to Bill Walton.

According to Bruce, there was only one man capable of soothing an angered Keese.

"When he got mad, the only guy who could calm him down was 'Mooney' [Billy Knight]," Bruce said. "But we had a lot of fun with Lucius. He was really a good guy to be around. When we wanted to have some fun with him, it usually centered around doing something to make him mad, then getting out of the way!"

Knight Wanted to Stay at Home

Braddock (Pennsylvania) High School's Billy Knight could have punched his ticket for virtually any college in the country when he

*Billy Knight led the Panthers in scoring and rebounding for three
straight seasons (1972-1974).*
Photo courtesy of the University of Pittsburgh Athletic Department

was being recruited during the 1969-1970 basketball season, but
several factors helped keep him in Pittsburgh.

"I knew that I wanted to stay at home," said Knight, who in
2004 was the general manager of the NBA's Atlanta Hawks. "I'm

from a large family. I hadn't been away from home and wasn't interested in doing it."

That didn't keep the schools from courting the six-foot-six, smooth-shooting forward.

"I took my visits," he said. "I visited NC State and Syracuse. All the schools were after me—North Carolina, West Virginia, Arizona State, Jacksonville, but I knew that Pitt was getting a lot of local guys. I thought that was special. That was something different. Those were important factors in my thinking."

One of Knight's former high school teammates, Carl Morris—who was a year older than Knight—was on the Pitt roster during the process.

"I had been to a lot of Pitt games before college," Knight said. "I'd been on campus, spent a lot of time with Carl there."

Knight remembers the effect his Pitt coaches had, not only during his recruitment, but later in life.

"Coach [Tim] Grgurich was a big part of my recruitment," Knight said. "He was the main guy, the coach I spent most of my time with, and knowing what type of man coach [Buzz] Ridl was and coach [Fran] Webster was made a big difference."

As a senior, Knight led the Panthers to a school-record 22-game winning streak and a spot in the Elite Eight of the NCAA Tournament.

"I wouldn't trade my experiences at Pitt for the world," he said. "I'm happy that things worked out the way they did."

There Used to Be Some Basketball Players Here

From 1969 to 1977, Pitt's basketball program signed 10 players from the Pittsburgh City League to scholarships. Darelle Porter signed with Pitt in 1987, but he remained the program's only City League signing through the 2003 recruiting class.

Tim Grgurich, who grew up Lawrenceville—a Pittsburgh city ward—established the urban pipeline in the late 1960s. He was primarily responsible for recruiting Chris Jones, Cleve Edwards, Frank Boyd, Kirk Bruce, Sam Fleming, Melvin Bennett, Wayne Williams, Kelvin Smith, Sonny Lewis, and Sam Clancy. To further illustrate the caliber of scholastic talent in the city then, consider a few of the players—Ken Durrett, Maurice Lucas, Rick Coleman, and Larry Anderson—who left Pittsburgh to play college basketball at the Division I level.

"I only came to Pitt because of Gurg," said Edwards, who starred at Fifth Avenue High School before enrolling at what was then Robert Morris Junior College. "I said to him, 'Why are you working hard to recruit me, a guard, when what you need are big people?' But he just worked so hard at recruiting. I could not say 'no' to him."

"He was the chief recruiter," Bruce said. "He knew his way around the city, and he had a lot of friends. He knew Spencer Watkins at Schenley, Freddie Yee at Westinghouse. He had good relations with coaches all over this area. Back then, there weren't all these NCAA rules about the number of times you could contact a kid. He would come to my school [South Hills] every day. He would call you before a big game when you were playing in high school. He'd fire you up. When you got off the phone, you'd think, 'Hey, let's go!'"

"It was all Grgurich," said Clancy, when asked why he attended Pitt. "He's one of those guys you feel you can trust. You hear so much crap when you're being recruited, but he wasn't like that. He didn't promise me the world. He didn't tell me I would come in and start, but he told me that I probably could."

"It was a wonderful time period," said Grgurich, who resigned as Pitt's coach in 1980—after three straight winning seasons—because of squabbles with the school's administration. "We were able to start bringing city kids in to Pitt. Before, when Pitt was a private institution, we couldn't do that. We tried to get Kenny Durrett so badly. The earliest City League guys who came to Pitt [Jones and Edwards] had to go to Robert Morris [then a junior college] first."

One of Clancy's old City League rivals, Schenley's Sonny Lewis, already was a starter for the Panthers when Clancy arrived, but their college careers together lasted only a few months. Lewis transferred to Point Park College during Clancy's freshman season.

"We were rivals in high school, but we were close in college," Clancy said. "Sonny was one of the best players to come out of Pittsburgh. He was about six foot two, and he could do it all. He handled the ball, he could shoot, and he could jump with any big man. His vertical leap had to be 40-something. He was a remarkable player."

Lewis died from a drug overdose not too long after his college career ended.

Grgurich hit the pavement across western Pennsylvania in his search for players. Unlike in later years, the Pittsburgh area had been a fertile recruiting ground for major colleges.

"That's a mystery," he said, when asked why the region no longer produced many Division I prospects. "Sonny Vaccaro and I talk about that all the time. When I was coach at Pitt, and before that, western Pennsylvania was as good a place as any in the country, and you're talking about a smallish area, not like a New York, a Detroit, or a Washington, D.C."

It was a good thing that Pitt finally opened its doors to City League players, because Grgurich and other college coaches in the district waged harsh recruiting battles against outsiders.

"Back then, the ACC [Atlantic Coast Conference] raided western Pennsylvania," said Grgurich. "They killed us. Kids like Brad Davis, George Karl, Dick DeVenzio, all went to the ACC. I was a young coach, and I would really get pissed off about it."

It was a helpless feeling, to some extent, but one in which Grgurich and his chief competitors were kindred souls. Their recruiting options were limited.

"Nobody in Pittsburgh had the kind of money back then to go around the country and recruit," Grgurich said. "There was no Big East. We were all in the same situation. Everyone pretty much had the same budgets then. There was no TV, no Big East, no ESPN, no cable networks. Nike was just coming on the scene as far as shoe contracts, and that type of thing. When that happened, with all the television money and the Big East, college basketball in the East just exploded on the national level."

Grgurich suggests that maybe it was for the best that he left Pittsburgh for Nevada-Las Vegas in 1980.

"Our recruiting bread and butter was western Pennsylvania," he said. "If I had stayed at Pitt, and the area dried up the way it did, without the Big East, I don't know what I would have done."

Grgurich also was the first Pitt basketball coach to start an all-black lineup. Sam Clancy, Sammie Ellis, Terry Knight, Wayne Williams, and Dwayne Wallace took the floor at Fitzgerald Field House for the start of the Panthers' 78-75 loss to Cincinnati on January 10, 1979.

Forget About the Bet, Coach Majors

It's a good thing for Pitt football that John Pelusi Sr. didn't insist that Johnny Majors pay up on a certain bet won at the Pelusi's Youngstown, Ohio, home in early 1973.

Majors had already been recruiting Pelusi's son, John, for Iowa State during the 1972 season, and when Majors took the Pitt job, he kept right on recruiting the player who would become the Panthers' starting center for their 1976 national championship season.

"My father had his own NCAA rules," Pelusi recalls. "Pick five schools to visit, and that's it. I told my dad that I was going to go for a visit at Pittsburgh, and he looked at me like I was crazy. 'They were 1-10 last year; they're terrible. Why do you want to do that?'"

But the young man was insistent, even if his father continued to have doubts. That's when Majors made his own visit—to Youngstown.

"My dad was just relentless on Majors," Pelusi said. "'That place was 1-10. He's not going there. I won't let him!'"

Mr. Pelusi and Coach Majors decided to settle the matter in a game of billiards. If Majors won, the kid would go to Pitt. If the father won, he could go elsewhere.

"Coach Majors ended up losing to my dad, but I ended up going to Pitt anyway," Pelusi said. "Coach Majors, when he's recruit-

*Brothers John (50) and Jeff Pelusi (51) were members of
Pitt's 1976 national championship team.*
Photo courtesy of the University of Pittsburgh Athletic Department

ing you, he makes you feel like you're the only one, the most important one."

Pelusi wasn't the only family member to play for the Panthers.
Brothers Jeff (linebacker) and J.C. (defensive lineman) soon followed, and all three played on nothing but winning teams during
their careers.

First One to the House Gets the Player!

Many high school seniors who are multisport athletes have had
to choose between accepting a scholarship to play college football or
signing a contract to begin a professional baseball career.

Johnny Majors's first recruiting class of 1973 included a stand-out baseball-football player named Robert Haygood, and he faced that enviable problem: a pro baseball opportunity with the New York Mets or a chance to play football at Pitt. Haygood, an East Point, Georgia product, eventually chose Pitt, but finished his career as a basketball player for the Panthers!

Haygood was recruited by Joe Avezzano, who had close ties to Florida and Georgia.

"We became tremendous friends during that whole period," Haygood said. "Initially, I was thinking about going somewhere on the West Coast, but he really got close to me as a person, and I felt good about the things he was saying, plus his actions."

As it turned out, the night that Haygood signed with Pitt was the same night the Mets offered him a deal to play pro baseball. Haygood had played in a high school baseball game earlier that evening.

"The guy from the Mets followed me home from the game," Haygood said. "I didn't even know they had anyone at the game, but Coach Avezzano knew. He followed me home, too. He probably thought, 'We're gonna end up losing this kid.' But once we got home, my dad was pretty stern about what he thought I should do. He was adamant about me going to college."

Haygood enjoyed a fine career as a quarterback/kick receiver for the Panthers, and became the team's No. 1 quarterback at the outset of the 1975 season, before splitting duties with Matt Cavanaugh. Haygood again was the starter when Pitt opened its perfect 12-0 season at Notre Dame in 1976, but his football career ended the following weekend when he tore cartilage in his left knee on a running play in a 42-14 win against Georgia Tech in front of family and friends at Grant Field in Atlanta.

"I didn't even know I was hurt until I tried to get up, and my leg just locked," he said. "Doctor [Jim] McMaster came out on the field and looked at it, and the knee was just like jello. That's when I knew I was in trouble."

Haygood, who had one more year of athletics eligibility because of the redshirt, rehabilitated himself to the point where he felt comfortable with the knee. He decided, however, to concentrate on basketball, a sport he had already been playing for the Panthers.

Pitt's Ralph McClelland (14), Larry Harris (hidden), and Robert Haygood (32) set a trap for West Virginia's Bob Huggins in the 1975 ECAC playoff game in Morgantown.
Photo courtesy of West Virginia University Athletics Archives

"Looking back, I probably should have tried to play football [in 1977]," Haygood admits. "It's something I've regretted."

The Other Player's Name Is Hugh Green

New Pitt football coach Jackie Sherrill and his assistants hit the recruiting road hard following the Panthers' 1976 national championship season. While watching film of a young Mississippi running back named Ray "Rooster" Jones, they couldn't help but notice a player on the other side of the ball, North Natchez High School's Hugh Green.

"I guess they liked what they saw," Green said.

That's an understatement. But first, Pitt had to pry Green from his home state. He had signed a Southeastern Conference letter of intent with Mississippi State.

"I wanted to stay in the SEC and within Mississippi," he said.

Pitt assistant coaches Don Boyce and Bob Matey convinced Green to visit Pittsburgh, and he was sold.

"I remember it was snowing," Green said. "When I came up, it was right after Pitt had won the national championship, so those guys were still around campus. I got the chance to meet Tony Dorsett, J.C. Wilson, Don Parrish, and Elliott Walker. I took a liking to J.C. The way Pitt recruited me was the same way we did it when I was there: The players took you around and told you straight. Coach Sherrill promised me one thing: that I would receive more publicity in one year at Pitt than I would in four years anyplace else."

Sherrill's Blunt Assessment

Jackie Sherrill gave high school football players a direct assessment of life on the Pitt campus when he was recruiting them.

"[Sherrill] told us up front what to expect," Mark May said. "He explained to us that Pittsburgh wasn't some quaint, little college town and that there would be a lot of diversions and social opportunities. But he talked to us and told us that he expected us to behave like men."

May and his fellow recruits were attracted to Pittsburgh at a vibrant time—for both the city and the school's football program.

"My recruiting weekend included Rickey Jackson and Hugh Green," May said. "Cecil Johnson, Don Parrish, and Tony Dorsett were our player hosts. They didn't normally take recruits around. Their attitude was like, 'Hey, we don't usually do this. You guys are coming here.'"

The players had a unique opportunity to experience what Pittsburgh had to offer.

"It was just a fun weekend," May said. "That was my first impression of Pittsburgh, that I'm visiting a program that's just won a national championship, and the Heisman Trophy winner is showing me around. What's not to like? I thought to myself, 'Why am I not coming here?'"

The players' trip from Greater Pittsburgh Airport to the Oakland campus also made an impression.

"At that time, they brought a lot of recruits in at night, so when you came through the Fort Pitt Tunnel, the city was all lit up," May said. "For me, coming from a small city [Oneonta] in upstate New York, it was very impressive."

Marino Picked Football Over Baseball

In February 1979, Central Catholic High School's Dan Marino signed a letter of intent to play football at Pitt. A few months later, baseball's Kansas City Royals made Marino their fourth-round pick in the amateur draft. Foge Fazio, the assistant coach most responsible for recruiting Marino, felt confident all along that Marino would end up at Pitt.

"Deep down, I always felt like Danny was coming to Pitt," Fazio said. "I wasn't too worried about it. Of course, you always think a school like Notre Dame might try to jump in and make a push. But Arizona State, Clemson, UCLA—the baseball schools—I thought they were the ones we had to be the most worried about. They played baseball the year round. Lots of times, kids who are good at baseball and football will think, 'Why should I get my head beat in playing football?'"

Fazio had been going to Marino's high school baseball games since 1977, the star prospect's sophomore year. Later, Marino and one of his Central (and later Pitt) teammates, Lou Lamanna, would make themselves visible on the Pitt campus.

"We used to bring him up to the [Fitzgerald] Field House and play basketball," Fazio said. "[Assistant coach] Joe Pendry and I would play against Danny and Lou. I don't know if they had NCAA regulations that strong back then. I'd have probably broken every one of them."

Marino did engage in serious negotiations with the Royals but ultimately decided not to pursue professional baseball. Fazio emphasizes the strength of Marino's support system at home.

"His grandmother was very influential," Fazio said. "His parents, too. Danny's dad did a good job with him. His mother worked as a crossing guard in their neighborhood."

The Pitt coaches received some outside help—in their own backyard—throughout the process.

"We took Danny down to Three Rivers Stadium to see [Pirates manager] Chuck Tanner," Fazio said. "They spoke in the clubhouse about his options. Bill Madlock talked to Danny a few times. He helped us recruit other guys, too. Phil Garner. The Pirates were good to us."

Vaughan Decided Against DePaul

Roy Chipman had replaced Tim Grgurich as Pitt's basketball coach following the 1979-1980 season, and he needed some players. Fortunately, Seth Greenberg—one of Chipman's new assistants—was familiar with a six-foot-five scorer in Mount Vernon, New York, named Clyde Vaughan.

"I went to Pitt because of Seth Greenberg," Vaughan said. "I was all set to go to DePaul, where Ray Meyer was coach. I had known Seth from Five-Star Camp. He and Coach Chipman said to me, 'Come and visit.' I said, 'No, Coach, I'm going to DePaul.' But they kept after me. I visited Pittsburgh, saw some people that I knew and really liked the place. Everything just came together, and I felt this was the best place for me."

Vaughan became a three-year starter and is one of Pitt's all-time leading scorers. He has no regrets.

"Pitt was the best four years of my life," he said.

Even though Vaughan later went to the University of Connecticut as an assistant coach, he admitted his true feelings during a 2004 interview.

"Even though I'm a UConn coach now, I'll always be a Panther," he said.

Lion Lover Fralic Became a Panther

Bill Fralic admits that, when he was a youngster growing up in suburban Pittsburgh, he usually rooted for Penn State when it played Pitt.

"As a young kid, I had an affinity for lions," Fralic said. "Typically, the ones in Africa, but that kind of carried over to the Detroit Lions and the Penn State Nittany Lions. They were closer to real lions than panthers were."

Luckily for Pitt, those feelings weren't much of a factor when Fralic was arguably the nation's most coveted scholastic lineman during the fall of 1980. Offers came from everywhere for the six-foot-five, 270-pound tackle.

"I didn't know where I was gonna go," he said. "Part of me thought I wanted to go somewhere far away into the sun, like California or Miami of Florida. But the other part of me wanted to go to a school with a good football program. At the end of the day, I guess I was conflicted. When it all came down to it, I knew in my gut that the best move for me was to go to the University of Pittsburgh. It had a great program at the time [coming off back-to-back 11-1 seasons], with great coaches. There were guys there who I had played with in high school. I could still be away from home but close enough where my friends and family could see me play."

Jackie Sherrill retired from coaching in 2003 after 26 seasons. He once said Fralic was the only offensive lineman he'd coached who was good enough to come in and be a starter from the first day of practice as a freshman. Fralic remembers the first time he came in contact with the man who was to be his head coach for only one season (1981) at Pitt.

"I caddied for him a golf function at Alcoma [Country Club]," Fralic said. "This was the summer right before I was going into ninth grade. [Sherrill] asked me when I was reporting for football practice or where I went to school, something like that. Alcoma is right over the hill from Linton School, which at the time was the school for ninth and tenth grades at Penn Hills. You could literally point from the golf course to the school, and I told him I was going there. He was shocked."

Fralic became an All-American at Pitt. Curiously, the man who played an important part in Fralic's development as a player, offensive line coach Joe Moore, didn't influence Fralic's college choice. Another assistant, Joe Naunchik, was the man primarily responsible for his recruitment.

"I didn't base much of my decision on the fact that Joe Moore was the line coach," said Fralic. "As it turned out, it might have been the most significant part of my experience, because he was, without a doubt, one of the finest coaches I've ever been around."

Moore, who died in 2003, impressed Fralic in many ways.

"I owe a lot to him," Fralic said. "He affected a lot of guys in a great way that went way beyond football. He was very rough around the edges, but he had a heart of gold, and he really made guys want to be the best they could be. He enjoyed what he did, and we had a lot of fun along the way."

Saving the Best for Last

The last football scholarship the Pitt coaching staff extended in 1999 went to a player virtually by default. Coach Walt Harris explains:

"We had a commitment from a junior-college receiver," Harris said. "Our receivers coach went to sleep on him and didn't work him. The kid ends up going on another visit, and we didn't even know about it."

A former Pitt graduate assistant coach, then working in California, called the Pitt coaches with that bit of information.

"By then, it was too late," said Harris. "The kid really liked the other school. The school was a bigger name than us. He went to the same high school as [Pitt receiver] Latef Grim."

When it became clear that the Panthers had no chance to sign the prospect, they turned their attention toward a high school senior from Florida, Antonio Bryant.

"We called Antonio on the Sunday or Monday before Signing Day and told him we wanted him," Harris said. "His feelings were hurt because we didn't tell him that on his visit. As we found out later, he could be very, very emotional. He didn't sign with us until later in the afternoon because he flip-flopped around between Louisville and us. But he wanted to play against Miami. That was his thing. It's interesting, because he had his worst games against Miami. He did not perform well, because he was trying too hard."

Bryant did star for the Panthers from 1999 to 2001 and earned the Biletnikoff Award in 2000 as college football's best wide receiver.

"Recruit to Shoot"

Ben Howland replaced Ralph Willard as Pitt's basketball coach in March 1999. He came to Pittsburgh following a successful stint at Northern Arizona, where his later teams were among the nation's leaders in three-point shooting. At his hiring, Howland talked about his coaching philosophy, which included the creed, "Recruit to shoot."

Eighty-nine wins later, Howland departed Pitt to take over at UCLA, and most of those victories resulted from outstanding defense, mental and physical toughness, plus inspired play and leadership from the point guard position.

"That's what I had used before," explained Howland, one year after leaving Pitt. "We were looking for a catchphrase to sell and recruit. Usually, kids like to shoot. The reality is, you recruit to defend, recruit to be physical, recruit to be tough. Every place has its profile kid, and you have to change a little bit."

Howland knows one thing for sure: He can take pride in the basketball program he established at Pitt.

"I'm really proud of what I helped start there," he said. "We'll always be grateful to [athletic director] Steve Pederson and chancellor [Mark] Nordenberg for the opportunity."

Keeping Tabs on Fitzgerald

Larry Fitzgerald pledged his intention to attend Pitt following his graduation from high school, but academics forced him to enroll at Valley Forge (Pennsylvania) Military Academy for his first year after high school. Some college recruiters took that to mean that the young wide receiver was open game when Signing Day approached the next year.

"A lot of other schools came in at the last minute, including Notre Dame and Tennessee," Fitzgerald said. "They had backed off earlier because of my grades situation back home. They were trying to get back in."

Walt Harris and his staff had to be more than anxious when Fitzgerald decided to make some college visits around that time, including one to Ohio State.

"I wasn't doing anything on weekends [while in prep school], so I wanted to go out and take a look and see what the other schools had to offer," Fitzgerald said. "As I went there, though, it kind of reaffirmed my commitment to the University of Pittsburgh."

While Fitzgerald was going to visit schools, Pitt assistant Curtis Bray was making a regular trek to Valley Forge.

"I saw Coach Bray every week," Fitzgerald said. "The whole Pitt coaching staff was very understanding about the things I wanted to do in terms of my visits."

Big Apple Helps Produce Big East Titles

Although western Pennsylvania supplied basketball talent for Pitt's teams for much of the 1970s, a larger, more fertile recruiting territory helped produce many of the players for the Panthers throughout the 1990s and into the next century.

Those Pitt basketball rosters became dotted with players who called the Big Apple home. George Allen, Andre Williams, Andre Alridge, Orlando Antigua, Jerry McCullough, Eric Mobley, Jarrett Lockhart, Jaime Peterson, and Ricardo Greer all chose to come to Pittsburgh for their college careers. Another group, including point guard Carl Krauser, forward Mark McCarroll, and center Chris Taft, however, were poised to make the greatest impact of any.

"Some of the attraction to Pittsburgh is the fact that it is a city, and it is an urban environment, which these guys are comfortable with," said Barry Rohrssen, also a New Yorker and the Pitt assistant coach chiefly responsible for recruiting the New York-New Jersey area. "They come to a place where they still see buildings and feel concrete underneath their feet. Plus, the [Big East] conference gets so much exposure. Even if they didn't know where Pittsburgh is, or have never been there, they know it's on the radar screen, know that it's in the Big East."

Although nowhere near the size of New York City, the urban lure of Pittsburgh can be a blessing, especially to college basketball coaches and players.

"I just liked being in the city," Krauser said. "Pittsburgh is kind of a smaller version of New York. You can't live the fast pace all the time, but you can be somewhere near it."

The close proximity is something that Rohrssen uses as another selling point. "If we can get a kid from New York to visit us, he understands that it's not a difficult trip. It's an easy flight, and it's not that bad a drive."

Taft, who enjoyed a tremendous freshman season (2003-2004), knew next to nothing about Pitt while growing up, but he came to appreciate what Rohrssen meant.

"The only person I knew about from Pittsburgh was [former Panther All-American] Charles Smith," Taft said. "When they started recruiting me, I got to meet him. I really didn't know that much about Pittsburgh."

Nor, it turns out, did he know much about some of his future teammates, considering the size of New York City and the number of basketball players there.

"I knew about Mark McCaroll and Carl Krauser when I got to the eleventh grade," Taft said.

By then, his thought processes also began to change.

"When you're young, everybody wants to go to a North Carolina or a Duke," he said. "The only team I focused on when I started playing ball, when I was 12, was Duke. That's where I wanted to go. Then, as you get older and start thinking more, you realize it'll be real good to play in front of your own fans. Pittsburgh wasn't that far away. This was just a great fit for me."

Pitt's magnificent Petersen Events Center also helped lure the highly touted big man. Taft visited Pitt in the summer of 2002, a few months before the Panthers began playing in their new home.

*Carl Krauser (left) and Chris Taft, two members
of Pitt's New York City connection.*
Photo by IMAGE POINT PITTSBURGH

"He wound up visiting us first," Rohrssen recalled. "The two of us walked out on the court together—and he'd played in some big places, like the [North Carolina] Dean Dome—and he looked around. You could just see it in his eyes. He really liked the building. As the visit went on, he felt like this program was an extension of his high school, because it was so family-oriented, so comfortable."

Ricardo Greer and New Jersey's Brandin Knight actually steered McCarroll to Pitt.

"Ricardo was a New York guy, and everyone knew who he was," Rohrssen said. "Mark and Brandin Knight played together at an All-

Star game in Chicago, so that chemistry and camaraderie have been a big part of what we have here."

Krauser, who was recruited heavily by Temple, Duke, and Hofstra, had a similar feeling about Pitt.

"It looked like everybody stuck together here," he said. "I wanted to be a part of that."

The successful recruitment of Krauser is a story in itself, considering that Knight already had a firm grip on his position with the Panthers.

"It was difficult for us to recruit point guards at that time, because everybody saw Brandin as an obstacle, rather than an ally," Rohrssen explained. "Carl is a good player in his own right, and Brandin was ahead of him, but Carl still signed on and said, 'I want to be a good player in a good program. It's not as important for me just to go somewhere and have the ball in my hands from Day One.'"

Rohrssen, like many Pitt fans, appreciates Krauser's competitive spirit.

"When he signed on, one of the things he told us was, 'I want to help make this not just a good team, but a great program,'" Rohrssen said. "Those are the kinds of guys you want to have. You need somebody who has some heart and some fight in him. When you're going to play in front of 30,000 people at the [Syracuse] Carrier Dome, or at Madison Square Garden, Rutgers, those kinds of places, you need guys who are tough, mentally and physically."

The New York City connection has been self-sufficient. Players who go through the program talk to their friends and family members back home, and the good word travels truthfully among Pitt's players—past, present, and future.

"I've always believed that your players are your best recruiters, because they're not gonna lie to the guys coming in," Rohrssen said. "I'd rather the players tell a recruit how practice is, how campus life is, how the classes are. A lot of times, recruits get fed the same lines over and over by coaches who, basically, are selling the same product—a basketball program. It's really the kids who are living it every day who can give the best answers. Then we get feedback from our players after the visits, to find out how they think the recruit would fit in. I trust people like Julius Page, Jaron Brown, and Chevy Troutman, implicitly."

CHAPTER FIVE

HUMOR

The Gunner and Jock Sutherland

There is one story, mostly apocryphal, that Bob Prince, long before his days as a baseball announcer, raised the ire of Jock Sutherland during one of the Pitt football team's trips to Pasadena for a Rose Bowl contest.

Prince, who was an excellent swimmer and diver in his youth, attended Pitt briefly and was a varsity swimmer. One of his contemporaries was Pittsburgh's Hyman Richman, later a teacher at Pitt. Prince and Richman had been classmates and teammates at Schenley High School, just down the road from Pitt's upper campus.

"The Pitt football team is out in Pasadena," Richman said. "Bob showed up at the hotel where Pitt was staying, and he was wearing a Pitt varsity letter sweater. He went to the hotel bar and was drinking there in his Pitt sweater, attracting a lot of sportswriters. Sutherland found out about it and approached him and told him he had no business wearing that sweater. Prince told Sutherland he had earned that sweater fair and square as a varsity swimmer at Pitt. Sutherland was fuming, but Prince didn't care. He told the sportswriters that Sutherland was a lousy coach."

Smoking Discouraged on Campus

Doc Carlson, Pitt's longtime basketball coach who was a physician by profession, never hesitated to offer his opinions and advice to students on Pitt's campus.

"I remember him walking around campus in his white lab coat," Alex Kramer said. "If he saw a student who was smoking, he would stop to give them a lecture about the dangers of smoking, and this was well before anything was said or written about the health problems involved."

"He'd scream at you," Bimbo Cecconi said. "He hated cigarette smoking. He'd lecture complete strangers about it anywhere—on the street, in an elevator—you name it. 'You dumb such-and-such.'"

Carlson had a more discreet bit of advice for Pitt's incoming male freshmen, according to Cecconi.

"At freshman orientation, he would tell the kids, 'Stay with masturbation,'" Cecconi said. "'It's enjoyable, it's not harmful, and you're not gonna get in any trouble. You won't get any disease, and you'll be a happier guy for it.'"

On the Road with Doc Carlson

With Doc Carlson Pitt's Panthers knew to expect the unexpected and then some. From 1922 to 1953 Pitt basketball players were under the thumb of the eccentric and colorful coach Henry Clifford Carlson. Whether it was his legendary personality, his fondness for road games, or his strict on-the-court strategy and practice guidelines, Doc Carlson is a character whose place is secure in Panther lore. There aren't enough adjectives to describe Carlson, but former player Bimbo Cecconi tried.

"Gregarious, outgoing, friendly, loud, outspoken, critical," he said. "Throw in eccentric, too. Demanding. Tough. Old-school. Playing for Doc Carlson was a very unusual experience.

Pitt's one and only Henry Clifford "Doc" Carlson.
Photo courtesy of the University of Pittsburgh Athletic Department

"One time my mother came to a game. Doc took me out of the game. Afterward, my mother says to me, 'He's such a nice man. He put his arm around you when you came out.' I said, 'Mom, he was cussing me out!' Doc knew every four-letter word in the book, and then a few more. He used to call me a 'Black-Hander' [in reference to an old Italian extortion ring that preyed upon poor Italian immigrants in the United States].'"

Cecconi, who came to Pitt on a football scholarship in 1946, made a modern-day parallel to what it was like.

"That television program, *Survivor*, would have been perfect for Doc Carlson," Cecconi said. "He'd have you out of there real fast."

His bombastic behavior was not confined to the privacy of the sidelines, practice, or team meetings. When Carlson showed up, courtside was his stage for some of the most outlandish behavior. During the Pitt-Penn State game on January 21, 1950, Doc Carlson put on a memorable show.

"During the game, Doc went up in the crowd and started tossing bags of peanuts to the fans," Cecconi said. "He had a babushka. He put it on, then went up and sat with the organist. They used to have an organist at Penn State. That game was the most obnoxious one we ever went through with him."

Carlson's on-court antics were outrageous enough to sometimes cost the Panthers a win. Two technical fouls against Carlson led directly to a 47-45 loss at Denver during the 1948-1949 season.

"The basketball court there was up on a stage, so the playing floor was elevated from where the benches were," Cecconi recalled. "Doc was upset by a call late in the game. He took all of our clothes and threw them up on the court. He said to one of the officials, 'You've taken everything else from us. Here, take our clothes, too.'"

Even the opposing fans contributed to Carlson's act. On March 1, 1948, during a 52-36 loss at West Virginia, one fan, seated on the balcony level, emptied a bucket of water on Carlson. When the Panthers closed the season the following year in Morgantown, Doc came prepared.

"In the locker room, he put on a raincoat and boots," Cecconi said. "Then he opened an umbrella. That's how he led us to the court when the teams went out."

Pitt, on a late basket by Oland "DoDo" Canterna, had the last laugh, a 34-32 victory that shocked the Mountaineers and their fans.

"That old West Virginia Field House was a scary place," Cecconi said. "When the game ended, their fans were stunned. Doc says to the players, 'Go upstairs and get your clothes. Get your bags. We're getting the hell out of here. These SOBs are gonna kill us. We rode the bus back to Pittsburgh wearing our uniforms. That was the type of atmosphere he created with his personality. Still, [opposing fans] liked him."

Carlson also wanted his players to see the country and scheduled as many road contests as possible. The 1940-1941 Panthers, before Cecconi's time, opened the season with an extended road swing through the Midwest. Toward the latter part of that decade, Carlson and the Panthers played games in the Carolinas, Florida and California.

"We traveled like kings," Cecconi said. "We had 10 players, one coach, and one manager. That was it. We went in sleeper cars [in trains]. Doc would walk up and down the aisle. He'd bitch if you were playing cards or sleeping. 'This is a chance of a lifetime. You should be looking out at all this beautiful scenery. You'll never be able to afford a trip like this when you get older. Cecconi, you're nothing but a hobo from Donora, [Pennsylvania].'"

Road trips didn't stop Carlson from continuing to improve his team's basketball skills through impromptu and unconventional practice sessions.

"We had a 30-minute stop somewhere in Utah," Cecconi said. "We didn't have any basketballs, so we practiced with a couple of oranges that Doc pulled from his pockets. We're running around just outside the train, going through our plays, passing around an orange!"

On the road Pitt's basketball players—except Cecconi—had a particular reason, their coach, to never show up late at the dining car.

"I didn't realize why all the guys would go early to dinner," Cecconi said. "They didn't want to sit next to Doc. There was one big round table. I always sat next to Doc. That shows how naïve I was. The older guys knew better; they didn't want to put up with any of his stuff."

And while the players may have traveled like kings, the accommodations Carlson set up for their game at Loyola (in New Orleans) in 1947 were far from royal.

"To save money, Doc had six bunk beds set up at the gym at Loyola," Cecconi said. "We were sleeping in the gym! The next morning, we hear a basketball bouncing. It's Doc. He's standing there with boxes of doughnuts, milk, and juice. He said, 'We're gonna scrimmage another team here today. They're in town to play somebody else.'"

The other team featured a whiz-kid guard the Panthers couldn't stop.

"It was Bob Cousy and Holy Cross," Cecconi said. "Cousy, he was unbelievable. He was throwing passes behind his back. He embarrassed us."

Doc Carlson had a reputation for being a strict adherer to his own basketball philosophy. Carlson despised the zone defense, while Penn State's John Lawther was one of its leading proponents. That made for a combustible mix throughout most of the 1940s, when their respective teams met on a regular basis. The January 21, 1950, game where Carlson dished out peanuts to fans and sat with the organist also featured some odd activity on the court, because Carlson wanted to make a point.

"We held the ball, and Penn State wouldn't come out of the zone," Cecconi remembered. "We had little pockets in the shorts of our uniforms. People were throwing pennies out on the floor. We'd pick them up and just stick 'em in our pockets. At one point, Doc told me just to sit on the basketball, literally.

Penn State led at halftime, 5-0, with its center, Marty Costa, scoring all five points. Cecconi led the Panthers with seven for the game. The Nittany Lions won 34-21.

Carlson always kept developing his unique approach to the game, even if it meant altering the plan of attack against the home team. The night before a 1950 game at Memphis State, the Panthers players were preparing for bed at the Peabody Hotel.

"Next thing you know, we're paged," Bill Baierl said. "We get on a bus and go to some barn, where we practiced for about an hour. Doc Carlson puts in a new offense! He'd been thinking about doing it. He called it his 'Circle Offense.' Three guys ran counterclockwise and two guys went clockwise, and the ball never moved! Needless to say, we lost the game [53-39]."

The year before, during an extended trip to California, the Panthers went to see the Harlem Globetrotters play. Carlson had an idea.

"They were doing all those stunts," Baierl said. "When we got back to Pittsburgh, we were practicing them for a week before a game. We were sliding on our asses on that old stadium basketball floor. That's the game when Bimbo [Cecconi] jumped up on Ted Geremsky's shoulders and took the ball in the pivot."

Even Carlson's methods were too crazy for some of his own players.

"People couldn't put up with them," Cecconi said. "He got rid of a lot of good basketball players. You had to follow his rules. He was strict as hell. Me, I was just happy as hell to be there. He was a different type of person, but I got along okay with him. He liked me."

And stories about his unorthodox style and manner discouraged some local star athletes from becoming Panthers. Dick Groat was a Pittsburgh kid who starred in baseball and basketball during the mid-1940s. He could have gone to Pitt for basketball, but he chose Duke instead.

"I didn't want to play that continuity offense [an offense that emphasized running and passing, keeping the ball moving] that Doc ran," said Groat, who was the 1952 College Basketball Player of the Year. "He never had any big people, because he wanted players who could run his Figure Eight. I didn't want to play that style of basketball."

Carlson never cared what people thought. He stuck to his approach despite what his opponents did on the court and what the scoreboard showed at the end of the game.

"Everybody knew our plays," said Bernie Artman, who played for Pitt in the early 1950s. "He was using the same ones for 30 years. He used to say, 'Keep working it, keep working it. It'll work.' Well,

Bimbo Cecconi looks for a passing lane while atop Ted Geremsky's shoulders. The play was the brainstorm of Doc Carlson, who took the idea from the Harlem Globetrotters.
Photo courtesy of the University of Pittsburgh Athletic Department

it didn't work, and we struggled [at the end of Carlson's career].' I guess that's why they replaced him."

Carlson retired from coaching after the 1952-1953 season. His record at Pitt was 367-247. He was elected to the Naismith Memorial Basketball Hall of Fame in 1959. Still, his reputation and personality precede his accomplishments as a coach.

Doc Carlson died in 1964 at age 70.

That Dirty Field House

During the 1950s and 1960s, playing—and coaching—at the Pitt Field House could be a less than pleasurable experience.

"In those days, there weren't any restrictions on smoking," Panther Brian Generalovich said. "The Field House had a dirt track at the time. All the dust would rise throughout a game. Every five or six possessions, we would go over to the bench, and there would be wet towels set out for us. We would wipe our sneakers off because the dust was settling so much on the floor."

The sooty surroundings kept "Horse" Czarnecki's workmen on their toes.

"Each timeout, 'Horse' would have a crew come out with wide push brooms, covered with towels, to wipe off the court," Generalovich said. "Toward the end of the game it would be so smoky that there was a haze settled over the court. It was something to see."

Next Stop: Brentwood!

To hear Joe Schmidt tell it, Pitt's football players were hardly Big Men On Campus back in the early 1950s.

During his first three years on campus, Schmidt made the daily commute from his Mt. Oliver home to the Pitt campus in the Oakland section of Pittsburgh by trolley, or, as Pittsburghers like to say, street car.

Between classes, Schmidt and some of his buddies from the football team, young men such as Paul Blanda (George's brother), Charlie Yost, Eldred Kraemer, Lou Palatella, and Alex Kramer would congregate at one of the large wooden tables in the Commons Room area of the Cathedral of Learning. After practice, it was back home for Schmidt.

"A lot of times I'd fall asleep and go all the way to the end of the line at Brentwood," Schmidt said. "I ended up having to ask people to wake me up when we got to my stop. I got to know most of the conductors fairly well that way."

Not that the other commuters—or trolley conductors—were overwhelmed by the presence of the young football star.

"I was just another guy," Schmidt explained. "Nobody knew who the hell I was. Back then, you were a hidden commodity."

Tear Up That Scouting Report

As part of the preparation for Pitt's 1951 game at Michigan State, coach Tom Hamilton asked former Panther player and assistant coach Bill Kern to scout the powerful Spartans.

"I don't know why Bill Kern was asked to do it," said Alex Kramer, who sat in on the team meeting to hear Kern's analysis. "He was not on our staff at the time, but I remember what he said about Frank Kush, who was one of Michigan State's better players. 'You could push Kush this way, you could push Kush that way. He's lucky to have made first team in high school.' He demeaned Frank Kush's playing ability."

The Spartans, who ended that season 9-0 and No. 2 in the final national ranking, clobbered the Panthers 53-26.

"During the game, Kush was all over the field," Kramer said. "We couldn't stop him. Frank Kush was a superb football player. A little fellow, even for that time, but very quick."

Kramer introduced himself to Kush in May 2003 when both were in attendance at the College Football Hall of Fame induction ceremony in South Bend, Indiana, for among others, Dan Marino.

"I told him the story, and he had a good laugh," Kramer said.

Tappin' to Doc's Beat

Dick Lescott, who came to Pitt in the early 1950s and lettered in both basketball and baseball, remembers some of Doc Carlson's interesting practice and training methods.

"[Carlson] had a routine at different times throughout the season where you would run in place, and you had to count the number of times that your right foot hit the floor," Lescott said. "As a freshman, all of us guys with fuzzy beards—or no beards—we'd be trying like hell to make an impression of what good condition we were in."

But were they?

"The upperclassmen," Lescott said, "after they got to know you, said, 'You know, that's crazy [the way you freshmen are doing it]. He's looking for improvement from the beginning of the season to the end, so go slow at the beginning of the season, or during, so go slow at the beginning to make it look like you were making progress toward the end of the season.'"

"He called it 'The Fatigue Curve,'" Bimbo Cecconi said.

Hoops Manager Gets the Boot

Pitt basketball manager Alvin Markovitz had the dubious distinction of being ejected from a basketball game. The Panthers were playing at Westminster in 1954, and Markovitz was sitting at the scorer's table keeping the official book for his team.

"[Zigmund] Red Mihalik was officiating the game," Markovitz recalled. "He was a very demonstrative official. He'd be shouting, screaming, and waving his arms as if a foul was tantamount to murder."

It was a call Mihalik didn't make, however, that led to Markovitz's premature dismissal.

"The game was close, and [Pitt's] Dutch Burch faked out his man," Markovitz said. "He dribbled toward the basket and made a layup. He was hacked by Westminster's monster center and crumbled to the floor."

No foul was called.

"I couldn't believe it," Markovitz said. "I was so excited, I jumped up from the scorer's table. Screaming at the top of my lungs, 'Are you blind?!?! How can you miss that call?' Well, Red whirled around, stared at me, put his hands in the form of a 'T' and kicked me out of the ballgame."

The Panthers lost to the Titans 71-66.

"Pitt's Two Best Shot Makers"

Dr. Jonas Salk and Don Hennon—who later became a medical doctor—were two prominent figures known on Pitt's campus, if not to each other, during the late 1950s. Salk had discovered the vaccine for polio during research work at Pitt, and Hennon was lighting up scoreboards as an All-America basketball player for the Panthers.

Beano Cook, the school's sports information director, had an idea—to arrange for a photo of the two and send it around the country with the caption: "Pitt's Two Best Shot Makers."

"I kept trying to reach [Salk]," Cook said. "I left him messages but never heard back from him. So finally, one day I'm sitting at my desk, and the phone rings. 'This is Doctor Salk.' At the time, he was just so big, so famous, that I froze. But I explained to him what I wanted to do. I wanted to have the two of them pose for a picture outside the Cathedral of Learning. And you know what he said to me? He said, 'Who's Don Hennon?'"

Beano never did get the picture taken.

Iron Mike Riles Adolph Rupp

The University of Kentucky was looking for an opponent to close out its 1959-1960 basketball regular season. Pitt officials accepted the $5,000 guarantee to play the Wildcats in Lexington on March 5, 1960, providing legendary UK coach Adolph Rupp, the "Colonel," with a unique opportunity to watch Iron Mike Ditka play his brand of hoops.

"Kentucky's best play was to send its second guard around, come off a screen, and shoot," Pitt coach Bob Timmons said. "The first guard would come through and set a pick—on Ditka—in the corner or under the basket."

Ditka didn't take kindly to the pick and told Timmons about it during the next timeout.

"I told Mike I'd talk to the official," Timmons said. "I said, 'They're using an illegal screen down under the basket.' The official said, 'You know where you're playing, don't you? You're playing in Lexington, Kentucky, and you're playing the Colonel.'"

Timmons gave Ditka his instructions.

"I said, 'Ditka, the next time he comes over to set that screen, you go right through him,'" Timmons said.

Ditka did as he was ordered.

"The team benches were at the baselines," Timmons said. "This was right in front of Kentucky's bench. Ditka went through and knocked the Kentucky player off the court and over in front of their bench. Rupp looked at him and said, 'Ditka, you're nothing but a hatchet man.' And Ditka looked right at Rupp and said, 'Coach, you have a few pretty good ones on your team, too.' Rupp said, 'Hey, big boy, I'd sure love to have you here.'"

Football players moving over to play basketball at Pitt wasn't uncommon at that time, according to Timmons. Dick Deitrick, Charles "Corky" Cost, and Bimbo Cecconi were just a few of the football players who played another sport when football season was over.

"Many of them had played in high school, and they liked basketball," he said. "It was a different type of game. You got to handle the ball. That helped receivers, and you didn't have to worry about getting your head knocked off."

Football and basketball weren't Ditka's only sporting activities at Pitt.

"He has always been the quintessential Pitt athlete," said Jim O'Brien, who entered Pitt as a freshman when Ditka was a senior. "He was a starter in baseball, playing right field and catcher and, what people don't know, generally speaking, was that he was Pitt's intramural heavyweight wrestling champion. In the final, he defeated another football player, Ralph Conrad, from Altoona, who had been the PIAA [Pennsylvania Interscholastic Athletic Association] state champion. The Pitt wrestling coach, Rex Peery, said Ditka could have been an NCAA wrestling champion had he gone out for the sport."

Lost L.A. Weekend Had an Immaculate Twist

The Pitt basketball team made a memorable weekend trip to Los Angeles to play back-to-back games with UCLA and Pepperdine in 1972 on December 22 and 23.

On some trips, the travel party would use rental cars rather than a bus, so the Pitt players, coaches, and staff set out for UCLA and the first game of the swing. Broadcaster Bill Hillgrove was behind the wheel of one car, and his passenger manifest included coach Buzz Ridl, sports information director Dean Billick, star player Billy Knight, and another player.

"I got lost," Hillgrove said. "I made a wrong turn. I couldn't find Pauley Pavilion. I ended up taking the long route—a city street—instead of going on the freeway. We got to Pauley Pavilion 22 minutes before tipoff. All Billy had a chance to do was pull on his sneakers, take a couple shots, and it's time for the national anthem. Then he went out and poured in 37 points without any warmup."

The Panthers lost the game 89-73. UCLA was in the midst of its record 88-game winning streak at the time.

The next night, Pitt was scheduled to play Pepperdine, in Culver City. To wile away the time, Hillgrove and assistant coach Tim Grgurich turned on the television to watch the Pittsburgh Steelers-Oakland Raiders NFL playoff game from back in Pittsburgh.

"We were staying at the Sheraton Universal Hotel," Hillgrove recalled. "I remember Al DiRogatis and Curt Gowdy, who had been old AFL announcers, were doing the game on TV. They were really down after that play [The Immaculate Reception] by Franco Harris. When Ken Stabler scored right before that to make it 7-6, Oakland, one of them said that was the greatest drive in the history of professional football. Gurg and I looked at each other and said, 'Wow, was it that good?' But those two announcers were wounded souls when they signed off their broadcast that day, because their beloved AFL team had gone down the tubes."

The Panthers were unable to muster any similar magic against Pepperdine, dropping an 80-73 decision to the Purple Wave.

"What I remember about that night was that the preliminary game was a Pepperdine volleyball match," Hillgrove said. "There was probably more emotion for that than there was for the basketball game. That's when I realized how big volleyball is out there."

Take One for the Team, Schroeder

New football coach Johnny Majors instituted a demanding off-season conditioning program when he arrived at Pittsburgh in late 1972. More than a few players quit the program as a result. Majors's first recruiting haul included 76 players, and many of them came in handy during his first season (1973) with the Panthers.

"If we hadn't signed all those players, we wouldn't have had enough players to have a football team that first year," Majors said.

Just how thin Pitt's ranks were entering that era became clear the night before the spring football game at Pitt Stadium. Rod Kirby, who was first on the depth chart at one linebacker spot, was going to miss the game because there had been a death in his family.

"We didn't have any other linebackers," Majors said. "[Assistant coach] Jackie Sherrill called [assistant coach in charge of scouting] Keith Schroeder, woke him up early in the morning after he'd been up until about three o'clock. Jackie told him he was gonna have to play. Schroeder hadn't played in about two years, as our captain and linebacker at Iowa State. Schroeder played the whole damn game and didn't come out. That's how short-handed we were."

Strange Start to a Record-Setting Winning Streak

A long winning streak has to begin with the first one, and Pitt's 36-21 forfeit basketball victory at Rutgers on December 4, 1973, was strange, indeed.

Bill Hillgrove had a bit of an adventure just getting to the Rutgers campus.

"I was doing Chuck Brinkman's show at the time," Hillgrove said. "That's when I was a disc jockey at WTAE. Tom Whitman, the publisher of the *Latrobe Bulletin*, was a pilot, so he flew Jack Richards [father of Pitt point guard Tom Richards] and me up to Newark the day of the game."

Whitman, who wasn't much of a basketball fan, asked the people at Rutgers if there was a room in the basketball facility where he could get some sleep while the game was going on. He explained that he was a pilot who would be flying a private plane back to Pittsburgh later that night. Late in the first half, with Pitt holding a 36-21 lead over a Rutgers team that included Phil Sellers and Eddie Jordan, a fire alarm went off.

"Tom came running out of his room in his underwear," said Hillgrove. "People were exiting the building. That was quite a scene. Tom thought the place was on fire."

Out on the court, there was a fire of sorts. A group of African-American students had staged a sit-in on the floor to call attention to a cause.

"Hal Grossman was the lead official," Hillgrove said. "He did what he could. He sent both teams back to their locker rooms while the people sat on the court. Here we are, on the air, and we're trying to explain this protest. One of the people came around passing out a statement. I was getting ready to read it when I noticed the charged language in it. I said to myself, 'Don't read this on the air.' I paraphrased it and said, 'This is why they're protesting.'"

"They only had seats on one side of the floor at that facility," said Kirk Bruce, who started for Pitt that night. "It was during some stoppage of play. All of a sudden, these students start pouring out onto the court. Phil Sellers took the PA microphone and asked the kids to get off the court, but it didn't do any good."

As best as Hillgrove can remember, the protest had something to do with African-Americans' limited access to higher education.

"Finally, after about 15 or 20 minutes, Grossman came over to press row and said, 'As far as I'm concerned, this game is a forfeit to Pitt.'"

"We were downstairs in the locker room," Bruce said. "We wanted to keep playing. We were on a roll. We felt like we could wax them pretty good. Then, [assistant coach] Fran Webster came in and said, 'That's it; the game's over. We win.'"

Pitt continues to maintain the contest as a 36-21 victory. For many years, Rutgers did not list the game as part of its basketball records. Finally, Rutgers included the game in its basketball media guides as a loss, but without any score or game statistics. It also was Pitt's first victory in its school-record 22-game winning streak that season.

"If you were a college student back in the early '70s," Bruce said, "you came to expect that sort of thing."

"Tiger Paul"

A few seasons into Buzz Ridl's term as Pitt basketball coach, Frank Gustine Jr., Bill Baierl, and assistant coach Tim Grgurich found themselves in the stands at the Young Men's Hebrew Association (YMHA) in Oakland, watching a youth basketball tournament. One of the coaches, a chubby, 30-ish, balding gentleman, kept catching their eyes with his comical antics and unbridled enthusiasm. Constantly exhorting his players to give their best, the coaching wannabe spent an equal amount of time trying to keep his shirttail tucked in as he did shouting instructions to his players. The Pitt contingent briefly discussed the idea of bringing this character to its home games, where Panthers basketball—in the early 1970s—drew little in the way of fans or enthusiasm. Thus, the iconic "Tiger Paul," a.k.a. Paul Auslander, was created.

"I approached him and told him what we had in mind," Gustine said, "and he said he'd be glad to do it."

For most of the 1970s "Tiger Paul" made Pitt basketball games a hoot with his colorful costumes and courtside pranks. He was Pitt's most visible cheerleader in his standard fare—a long-sleeved shirt under a navy blue Pitt letter sweater, borrowed from Gustine—and occasionally some novel outfits, including pajamas and a Santa Claus suit. No matter his getup, he got everyone into the game.

"He'd run up and down the sideline and do the 'Let's Go Pitt!' cheer, and the students just went crazy," said Tom Richards, a former Pitt basketball player. "I can visualize it like it was yesterday."

But the routine appearance of "Tiger Paul" at the games was the result of some negotiation. Auslander, who made his daily living as a newspaper deliveryman, moonlighted by providing scores of sporting events to bookies around Pittsburgh. By accepting the Pitt opportunity, he would be sacrificing his extra income during the winter. The Pitt boosters fixed that.

"Frank and I each paid him $10 a game to make up for the money he lost," Baierl said.

And that wasn't the only perk.

"I had to drive him to and from the games at the Field House," Gustine said. "That was with my family in the car. I don't think he ever had a driver's license."

Free rides to the games and a steady paycheck for making people laugh. What more could a guy who spent high school as the punch line to fellow students' gags want?

"He had a lot of heart, but no talent [at football in high school]," said sportswriter Bob Smizik about his classmate at Peabody High School. "He was always the butt of jokes. He was a massive San Francisco Giant fans. One day someone slapped him on the back and left a taped sign—'I hate Orlando Cepeda'—on his back, which he walked around wearing most of the day."

Not only did the tomfoolery in high school prepare him for his one-man comedy troupe on the sideline, his famed moniker has its roots there as well. One day at football practice, while trying out for the team, the coach tried to inspire the five-foot-four, 181-pound Auslander to attack the blocking sled with more gusto.

"C'mon Paul," the coach said. "Hit that thing! Be a tiger!"

And what began as tiger-like encouragement was propelled into panther-like stardom. "Tiger Paul" attacked his role as sideline comedian with the vivacity of all of the Three Stooges. For example, in the 1973-1974 season opener at West Virginia—a game Pitt lost just before winning 22 straight—a referee admonished him for his outlandish behavior. Auslander, who was sitting at the end of the Pitt bench throughout the game, responded by shaking his behind at the official. The following year, during Pitt's victory against Temple at the Penn Palestra in Philadelphia, he was ejected from the premises.

"He had a thing where he could fall straight backward without hurting himself," Gustine said. "He was upset by an official's call and did that. He got tossed."

(His crazy antics weren't always limited to Pitt basketball games. An avid and emotional gambler, this astonishing legend about "Tiger Paul" persists: He once *flew* to Cleveland so he could *listen* to an Indians game on which he'd placed a bet. Another time, in a story "Tiger" told, upon returning home from a college basketball game a

"Tiger Paul"—and Frank Gustine's Pitt varsity letter sweater.
Photo courtesy of the University of Pittsburgh Archives

loser, he phoned the FBI and urged it to conduct an investigation into what he believed to be corrupt officiating.)

"Tiger Paul" also dabbled informally as a talent scout for Pitt basketball on at least one occasion. Tom Richards, who became a four-time letterman and the starting point guard for Pitt's Elite Eight team of 1974, was in his junior year at Moon (Pennsylvania) High School when *he* was discovered—by "Tiger Paul."

"Out of the blue, I get a phone call one day from this guy who says his name is Paul Auslander," Richards said. "He wants to know if I want to play on a team he's coaching in the Maccabiad Tournament. I agreed. My dad and I went to the Jewish Y, where the games were being played. This is the first time we ever saw 'Tiger.' My dad looked at me and I could tell he was thinking, 'You're out of your mind to play for this guy.'"

The younger Richards held his ground and then joined his "Tiger" and teammates in the locker room.

"'Tiger' handed out the uniforms," Richards said. "We're sitting there, and he's reading off a piece of paper what he wanted us to do in the game. My dad said to me, 'What have you gotten yourself into?' But, to make a long story short, we won the [Maccabiad Tournament]. It's hilarious. That was really the thing that put me on the radar screen, because I won the MVP award. I can always say that I played for 'Tiger Paul.'"

His fierce dedication to the team was also evident no matter where the team or any Pitt team was. During Roy Chipman's first season (1980-1981), "Tiger Paul" rode a bus for two days to watch the Panthers play Idaho, then North Carolina, in El Paso, Texas, in the opening rounds of the NCAA Tournament. An equal-opportunity unofficial cheerleader, he also made the trip to New Orleans at the end of 1976 to watch Pitt defeat Georgia in the Sugar Bowl, and win college football's national championship. Several days before the game, while strolling alone along Bourbon Street, a group of Pitt fans recognized him. A moment later, "Tiger"—arms flailing, fists punching—led an impromptu "Let's Go Pitt!" cheer.

But not everyone understood the "Tiger Paul" sideshow. Pitt's unofficial cheerleader delivered a personal message to a former Pittsburgher just prior to the start of the 1974 NCAA East Regional final versus North Carolina State—on the Wolfpack's home court.

"When we ran out on the floor before the game, 'Tiger' ran over to [former Edgewood High School star athlete and then-NC State assistant coach] Eddie Biedenbach and said, 'Eddie, how ya doin'?'" Richards said. "He knew Eddie. The look on [NC State coach] Norm Sloan's face was priceless. It was like he was saying to Eddie, 'You mean you actually know that guy?'"

And the critics continued. Two nights earlier, during Pitt's victory against Furman at Reynolds Coliseum in Raleigh, "Tiger"—at the urging of another booster, Mike Rossman—dressed up in boxing shorts and donned a robe with the inscription "Tiger" on the back. That was how he led the Panthers out to battle against the Palladins. During the telecast, color commentator Bucky Waters, a former head coach at Duke and West Virginia, made a remark to the effect that that guy isn't playing with a full deck. "Tiger Paul," a sensitive type who brooded easily, heard about the remark and complained to Baierl.

"I happened to have a brand new deck of cards on me, so I told 'Tiger' he ought to go up to Waters before the game on Saturday [Pitt versus NC State in the East final] and show it to him," Baierl said.

"Tiger" did as he was told, handing the cards to Waters and telling him, "Here, count 'em; there's 52!"

"People made fun of 'Tiger,' but he did a lot that people don't realize," Grgurich said. "He brought enthusiasm to the Field House. Now, it's all about enthusiasm. Before, some folks looked down on that kind of stuff. Today, there's Dick Vitale and ESPN, kids dressing up crazy at games, people yelling and screaming on talk shows ... and so much of it's on TV."

This constant criticism and the sense that he was not wanted resulted in all good things coming to an end. And so did the "Tiger Paul" show at Pitt basketball games. "Tiger" decided he'd had enough and ended the tradition in true comic, no-holds-barred "Tiger Paul" style.

"He went up in the stands, in front of [then-athletic director] Cas [Myslinski] and threw down his sweater at Cas's feet," Gustine remembered. "Cas kind of smiled. By that point, he was probably happy to get rid of him."

Auslander's presence at Pitt games was an on-again, off-again thing after that, and he eventually moved away from Pittsburgh, settling in Nevada. He died in 1992.

We're Pitt Basketball Players, Sir

Life on the road can become mundane for a college basketball team, but it was anything but that when the Panthers visited Charlotte, North Carolina, to play Davidson on January 9, 1974. Having arrived in town the afternoon before the game, the Pitt players were on their own for dinner that evening.

"A bunch of us, maybe six or seven, went out to a restaurant that was just down from the hotel," said Jim Bolla, the starting center for the Panthers, who were 10-1 at the time. "There was me, Tommy Richards, Billy Knight, Keith Starr, Willie Kelly, Sam Fleming. What was funny was that it was two white guys and the rest black."

Nobody in the group was laughing about what happened next.

"We were just outside the restaurant fooling around, telling jokes, whatever," Bolla said, "when this big car—it was either a Cadillac or a Lincoln—pulled up. One of the guys threw a ball of paper at somebody. At the same time, a guy got out of the car with a woman. Somebody picked up the paper and threw it again, and it hit the woman by accident. We just stood there, frozen."

But not for long.

"The guy then went back to his car, reached in and pulled out a .45," Bolla said. "It looked like a cannon. He pointed the gun at us. Billy Knight was the first one in the restaurant. I think Keith Starr and I got stuck in the door trying to get inside at the same time. It was like *The Three Stooges*. Willie Kelly dived underneath a car."

All the players made it safely inside the restaurant, an establishment without any windows, Bolla remembers.

"The guy and the woman came inside and sat down in another area," Bolla said. "Then, a few minutes later, another guy—big, ugly, nasty-looking—comes in and sits down and just orders coffee. He stared at us the whole time. Mooney [Billy Knight] said, 'That's it; I'm getting mine to go.' Finally, I said that I was gonna go over and talk to the guy who was with the woman."

The story gets better.

"I was looking around the corner to where he was sitting, and I was peeking back and forth to get him to notice me," Bolla said. "I went over and told him that we were basketball players from the University of Pittsburgh and that we were in town to play Davidson. I said how sorry we were for what happened, that we didn't mean to cause any trouble or inconvenience."

"Oh, you're a basketball team?" the man asked. "How good are you?"

"We're real good," Bolla said.

"Are you gonna win tomorrow?

"Yeah, we'll win."

"He asked me if we could get him some tickets to the game," Bolla said. "I said, 'Sure, no problem.' So we left the restaurant feeling a lot more relaxed. Back at the hotel I went to [coach] Buzz Ridl and asked him if I could get some tickets for this guy, and he said, 'Sure.'"

Following the game, a 90-63 win by the Panthers, the players noticed the man in the stands, waving his arms, trying to get their attention.

"Hey, why don't you come over to the restaurant now; I'll buy you all dinner," he said.

"We said, 'Well, we'll see,'" Bolla said. "Then, as we were walking out of the arena, another guy, a stranger, says to us, 'Hey, how do you know that guy?' We told him that we had met the night before at a restaurant. This guy tells us, 'That guy is one of the biggest bookies in town. He must have made a bundle tonight.'"

The incident did, however, have a sobering effect on the players, even with the happy ending.

"It was scary," Tom Richards said. "I was in a car with Keith Starr just after that happened, and we were noticeably shaken. I don't want to say we were naïve, but that type of thing wasn't something that was part of our lives. It was strange. It was the South. We didn't live there, so you didn't think about those things, but then you go down there and experience something like that—it was different."

Bonasorte Is Short One Tooth

Thousands of football players left their hearts and souls on the Pitt Stadium turf. Panther defensive back Chuck Bonasorte left one of his front teeth there on September 28, 1974—and went back to get it the next day!

The University of Southern California defeated the Panthers 16-7 that day, dominating the game with their superior size and strength. Bonasorte felt it early in the game, courtesy of a hit from USC defensive tackle Gary Jeter.

"It knocked about two-thirds of one of my teeth out," said Bonasorte. "I was coming off the field right after that, and one of the players told me, 'Man, you're really bleeding.'"

Bonasorte had special work done immediately to replace the tooth and was able to attend the film review meeting the next day. He saw the hit and had a thought.

"Al Romano and I went out looking for the tooth," Bonasorte said. "We found it, right where the play happened, on about the 35-yard line."

Dave Logan, Meet the Romanos

Middle guards Al Romano, a white kid from upstate New York, and Dave Logan, a black from the city of Pittsburgh, roomed together at the New Orleans Marriott while Pitt was preparing to play Georgia for the national championship on January 1, 1977. That's when the Romanos came for a visit.

"I said, 'Dave, do you mind if I have a couple of my family members up here to visit?'" Romano said.

"No, man, go right ahead," Logan said.

Al's father, Anthony Romano, was the first to arrive, followed by a non-family member, Tony Dorsett.

"Tony and my father had hit it off during our freshman year [1973]," Romano said. "He liked my father. He listened to him."

Then came the parade. Three brothers, a sister, and, finally, Dorothea—Al's mother—and there was no place to turn.

"Dave was sitting up on his bed, with his back to the backboard, and he crooked his neck to the right, toward the door," Romano said. "'Damn, how many more you gonna bring in here, Romano? You said a few.'

"I said, 'Dave, this is my family,'" Romano remembered. "'You want me to throw Tony out?!?!'"

Dave Logan followed Romano in Pitt's impressive line of outstanding nose tackles.

"I taught him everything I knew," Romano joked. "Dave was a quiet guy with a great smile—a good-looking guy. We used to talk about a lot of things. We didn't talk about football that much, but when we did, it was very matter-of-fact. He was very serious about learning as much as he could."

Bulldog Meyer and the Cracked Helmet

A smiling Carlton Williamson congratulated a beaming Glenn Meyer after the play, so it must have been funny.

Meyer, a five-foot-seven, 165-pound dynamo whose nickname was "Bulldog," walked on to Pitt's football team in 1976, a national championship season. He found himself on Pitt's kickoff coverage team when the Panthers shut out Tulane 48-0 at Pitt Stadium on October 29, 1977.

"The Tulane kid was going at 100 miles an hour, and I was going at 100 miles an hour, and there was a head-on collision," Meyer said. "I didn't even realize what had happened."

What happened was, Meyer cracked the right side of the helmet in a semi-circle around the top of the "Pitt" script.

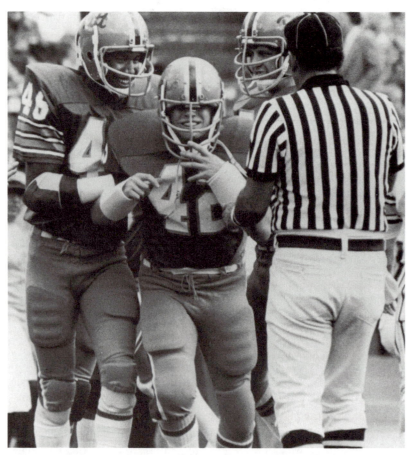

Carlton Williamson (left) congratulates Glenn Meyer following Meyer's
helmet-cracking hit against Tulane at Pitt Stadium in 1977.
Photo courtesy of the University of Pittsburgh Athletic Department

"Carlton Williamson came over to me, and he was smiling,"
Meyer said. "The helmet was down over my eyes, so I had to push
it up."

The broken helmet was good news for Meyer.

"On the sideline, one of the doctors came over and checked me
out," he remembered. "They were thankful it did crack. The helmet
absorbed most of the pressure, rather than my head."

The Flying Coach

On plane trips during Jackie Sherrill's five seasons (1977-1981) as Pitt's football coach, the head Panther—a licensed pilot—would pay a visit to the cockpit where he would sit and kibitz with the pilots. That did little to comfort Hugh Green and Mark May when they found themselves with a surprise air chauffeur one night after their junior season (1979).

Late one afternoon, Sherrill and his players flew by small private jet—not piloted by the coach—to central Pennsylvania for a Golden Panthers booster club function. The return trip provided a surprise.

"When we came back, Jackie flew the plane," May said. "It was a Cessna. We were all scrunched into it. We didn't know that he would be the pilot going back. None of us had ever flown with him, so we were all a little nervous."

More than a little nervous.

"Not a lot was said during the flight," May explained. "It was a white-knuckle trip, and we were happy as hell when that thing landed. I think we damn-near clapped. That was the first—and last—time I flew with Coach Sherrill as the pilot."

Winter in Moscow (Idaho)

The Pitt basketball team's reward for winning the 1982 Eastern Eight Championship Tournament was a trip to Pullman, Washington, to play Pepperdine in a first-round NCAA matchup.

"It was a rough trip," said Kimball Smith's, Pitt's basketball publicist. "We fly to Minneapolis, then to Spokane, Washington, then it's a long bus ride to Moscow, Idaho."

It wasn't a trip to remember.

"We were riding along, the players just staring out the windows," Smith said. "Nothing but winter wheat fields and mud. Everybody's wondering where the heck we are. Finally, the bus gets to the hotel. [Coach] Roy Chipman gets off the bus, looks around and says, 'Gentlemen, this isn't the end of the world, but you can certainly see it from here.'"

Pretend That Basketball Is a Coconut, Tico

The 1986-1987 Pitt basketball team brought a first-place trophy back to Pittsburgh after beating Kansas, Arkansas, and Wisconsin at the Rainbow Classic in Honolulu. Panther Ricardo "Tico" Cooper pocketed an extra $20 at the same time.

Cooper, who was from Aruba, South America, played junior college ball at Community College of Allegheny County (Pennsylvania) before transferring to Pitt. During the trip, the six-foot-seven, 235-pound Cooper bragged to his teammates how easy it was to climb a coconut tree, something he did all the time back home. An assistant coach offered Cooper $20 if he could do it.

"[Cooper] zipped right up, grabbed a coconut, and zipped right down," said Kimball Smith, who accompanied the team to Hawaii. "To see this guy go up that tree, using his feet and arms like a doggone native, that was really something to see."

Panthers Don't Like Gators and Snakes

Defensive line buddies Tony Siragusa, Marc Spindler, and Burt Grossman decided to bring some visitors to the weight room at Pitt Stadium one day in the late 1980s.

"They let their [python] snake and an alligator loose," teammate Bill Osborn said. "Whew! We all had to keep our eye on them. The alligator was maybe 12 or 18 inches, but it still had teeth. Everybody was lifting weights very gingerly for the next hour or so."

Heyward's Heisman Side Trip

As one of the five finalists for the 1987 Heisman Trophy, tailback Craig Heyward was invited to New York City for the formal announcement of the winner. The trip was extra special for Heyward, who was from Passaic, New Jersey, about a 40-minute drive from Manhattan, where the Downtown Athletic Club was located.

Among those accompanying Heyward to the Big Apple were Larry Eldridge and Linda Venzon from Pitts' sports information office, plus broadcaster Bill Hillgrove and cameraman Dan Pratt from WTAE TV. Hillgrove was planning to tape a segment with Heyward's high school football coach the day before the Heisman announcement.

"It was a pretty foregone conclusion that Notre Dame's Tim Brown would win it; still, it was a big honor to go up there," Eldridge said.

While preparing for the trip, Heyward had been telling the Pittsburgh contingent about a Passaic institution, a portable hot dog truck not too far from the high school.

"After Bill Hillgrove did the piece, Ironhead said, 'Hey, since we're in the neighborhood, why don't we go to the hot dog place I've been telling you about.'" Eldridge said.

It was late afternoon, and there was a special Heisman dinner to attend back in the city a few hours later, but the others decided to indulge Ironhead.

"The one [Heyward] ordered was called 'Whale of the Tail,'" Eldridge said. "It was a hot dog that had tuna fish spread on top of it and crumbled up bits of potato chips. He ate four of them!"

But Heyward was just getting warmed up. Next on the agenda was the formal dinner.

"I sat next to Ironhead, and I was absolutely amazed at how much he ate," Eldridge said. "It was surf 'n turf, steak and lobster, and he kept piling it in. Then he had dessert, and he ate mine, too."

When the dinner was over, one of the event coordinators told the players that, if they were hungry later in the evening, that they should feel free to order room service. The Downtown Athletic Club had rooms available, much like a hotel, to accommodate each of the five candidates and their travel parties.

"We find out the next day," Eldridge said, "that Ironhead [had] ordered up two bottles of Dom Perignon, and whatever else."

Heyward, who rushed for 1,791 yards that season, was noticeably bigger for Pitt's Bluebonnet Bowl game with Texas than he had been throughout the regular season.

"Between the end of his last regular-season game [Kent State] and the bowl, his playing weight jumped about 30 pounds," Eldridge admits.

Crash 'Em Kenny Bashioum

One of the most beloved figures around Pitt's football program since the early 1970s was Kenny Bashioum, a retired Pittsburgh steelworker who loved sports. Bashioum served a number of Pitt athletic directors and football coaches in a number of ways, from messenger to chauffeur. Everyone, it seems, has a story about Kenny B.

"During training camp at Johnstown, Kenny drove back and forth between there and Pittsburgh every day," said Ron Wahl, who was a member of the sports information office. "This one time, and he had to be well into his 80s, he was bringing a player down to the field for practice in his car, and he ran into a ditch and got his car stuck, right on the practice field. Everyone's saying, 'There goes Kenny B!'"

Hatfield in Hawaii

The Pitt football team played an unusual 12th game under strange circumstances to end the 1992 season.

Paul Hackett had been dismissed as coach in the days after a 57-13 loss at Penn State, and assistant coach Sal Sunseri, acting as interim coach, prepared the team for the game with the Rainbows. The Panthers lost the game 36-23, but at least one Pitt staff member remembers something that happened to John Hatfield, Pitt's intense, colorful, Jonathan Winters-lookalike equipment manager.

"There was a big collision near our sideline, and it turned into a fight, involving a lot of players," Ron Wahl said. "There were punches being thrown all over the place. It was a late hit out of bounds. Then, all of a sudden, John Hatfield—who was pretty intense and always good for a few laughs—stands up, and his slacks are down at his knees!"

Hatfield was a picture of calm under fire.

"He just got pummeled on the sideline," Wahl said. "I was in the radio booth at the time with [Bill] Hillgrove and Johnny Sauer at the time, and all of a sudden Hatfield stands up, pantless. He just nonchalantly reached down and pulled his pants up. He didn't even realize his pants were down around his ankles. He just pulled them up like nothing ever happened."

Managers Just Want to Have Fun

Looking for a way to kill time during the Pitt basketball team's stay at New York City's Marriott Marquis Hotel in March 1992, student managers Dave Kiehl and Steve Buchman decided to have some fun at the expense of some members of the Panthers' official travel entourage. The team was in the Big Apple for the Big East Championship Tournament.

"In most hotels, you could leave the message directly on the phone in that person's room," Kiehl said. "For whatever reason, at that time the person receiving the message had to come down to the front desk to retrieve it in person."

Kiehl and Buchman positioned themselves a few levels above the huge, atrium-style lobby at the Marriott and started making calls.

"We were able to look down and watch everybody come to the front desk to get their message," Kiehl said. "One person after another, including the coaches, would read the message, then have a look on their face as if to say, 'What the heck is this?'"

The managers saved their most ridiculous message for Les Banos, the team's excitable, Hungarian-born videographer and a former official photographer for baseball's Pittsburgh Pirates.

"We left a message for him that [football coach] Paul Hackett had called and that he wanted all the tapes from the defensive backs play for the last five seasons," Kiehl said. "He said he needed them right away to help prepare for the start of spring practice, which was right around the corner."

Banos fell for it.

"We found out later that Les made phone calls all across the country trying to find Paul Hackett," Kiehl said. "When he found out it was a prank, I never saw him any madder!"

Back in New York the following year, basketball coach Paul Evans showed the managers who was in charge while several members of the Pitt party were relaxing in the afternoon hours on March 13, 1993, the day a huge blizzard swept across much of the Northeast.

"We were having lunch in a restaurant next to the Dumont Hotel," Kiehl said. "The managers, some of the coaches, and their wives or girlfriends were there. In comes a gentleman asking for some volunteers to help push his car out of the snow. We all were capable of doing it, but we were nice and warm inside the restaurant."

Evans took charge of the situation, ordering all able-bodied men—himself included—outside.

"We all jumped when Coach Evans said, 'Let's go,'" Kiehl said. "He had a broken pinky finger at the time, so it was funny seeing him trying to push this car with his pinky finger extended in the air."

The incident, Kiehl explains, illustrated a side of Evans's personality that many fans never saw.

"A lot of people didn't get to know him too well, but he was a very giving person," Kiehl said. "He was very loyal to his friends."

Al McGuire's Fatherly Advice to Willard

Allie McGuire played college basketball for his father, Al, at Marquette during the early 1970s. Kevin Willard followed his father/coach, Ralph, to Western Kentucky—and later Pitt—in the 1990s. Ralph Willard understood the scenario and went to a fellow New Yorker, McGuire, for guidance.

"He said to me, 'If your son stinks, have him play for you because he's not gonna play and it won't make a difference, anyway,'" Willard said. "'If your son is an All-American, have him play for you. But if he's anywhere in between, don't let him play for you because of what people will say.'"

Ralph Willard admitted the situation probably affected a third party the most.

"It was probably more difficult on his mother than it was on Kevin," Willard said.

Ralph Willard remains the only Pitt basketball coach to have a son on his team.

Volunteer Needed for a Later Flight

Pitt's basketball players and staff sat on a jet at Pittsburgh International, preparing to fly to Chicago, the first leg of their trip to open the 1997-1998 season at Illinois State.

"We're sitting on the plane, and coach [Ralph] Willard still hasn't gotten on," said Tony Salesi, the team's trainer. "He was always late like that. He couldn't find his ticket or something. Then, on the intercom, we hear, 'Could we please have a volunteer to get off this flight so the head coach from the University of Pittsburgh can get on?' Guess who gets off? Dot, Ralph's wife."

Dot took a later flight but had connection problems, which meant she didn't arrive in Normal until around 5 a.m. the next day. Later that evening, Pitt dropped its season opener 87-65.